About the Book

Here are the fascinating stories of some inspired and dedicated Americans who contributed priceless gifts to the life of the nation but who have been forgotten in the rush of history. Author Vernon Pizer has delved deeply into the lives of these people with their bursts of genius, their audaciousness and vision, their persistent tinkering and experimenting.

Dr. Sara Josephine Baker became a physician when it was almost impossible for a woman to attain that role in society and, through her compassion for slum-dwellers, made outstanding contributions in the field of public health. James Buchanan Eads pitted himself against the raw power of the mightiest of rivers, boldly and brilliantly shaping the elemental forces into servants of society. Frederic Tudor endured ridicule and jail in a remarkable struggle that eventually made Yankee ingenuity admired from Calcutta to Rio. Dr. Charles R. Drew, refusing to be defeated by rebuffs because he was a black, persisted and ultimately triumphed in a medical breakthrough that has saved countless thousands of lives. These and many others are brought vividly to life in this book.

SHORTCHANGED BY HISTORY
America's Neglected Innovators

by VERNON PIZER

MEDIA CENTER
CASTILLERO JUNIOR HIGH
SAN JOSE, CALIFORNIA

illustrated by
Catherine Stock

G. P. Putnam's Sons · New York

Library of Congress Cataloging in Publication Data
Pizer, Vernon.
   Shortchanged by history.
   Includes index.
   SUMMARY: Discusses the lives and contributions
of little-known inventors in American history in-
cluding Joseph Jenks who invented a more efficient
scythe and James Buchanan Eads who completed and
launched the first ironclad in American waters.
    1. Inventors—United States—Biography—Juvenile
literature. [1. Inventors] I. Title.
T39.P59   609'.2'2 [B] [920] 78-24141
ISBN 0-399-20665-5

PRINTED IN THE UNITED STATES OF AMERICA

Contents

SHORTCHANGED BY HISTORY
America's Neglected Innovators

1
Forgotten Weavers
of the American Fabric

The tissue of the Life to be
We weave with colors all our own . . .
—John Greenleaf Whittier

THE FABRIC OF AMERICA HAS BEEN woven by many hands—old hands and young, white, black, brown, yellow hands. Gnarled and calloused or soft and manicured, male or female, delicate or strong, each in its own way contributed to the shaping of the national design.

But in every generation from the very beginning of the American experience there were some whose hands were more sensitive or more innovative. Some had more notable qualities of mind or spirit. Some left a larger, clearer imprint than the others on the fabric of the nation. Throughout its history the land has been peopled by those who strive, who seek, who dream grand dreams. Every generation has produced a special few who find a way to flesh out those dreams to give them life and substance.

It was those "fleshers of the dreams"—with their bursts of genius, their inspired, persistent tinkering and experimenting, their boldness in venturing where none had trod before them—who enhanced the quality of life. They created the processes and devices that elevated the country into its commanding position among the family of nations. These were the Benjamin Franklins, Robert Fultons, Eli Whitneys and many others. The list is long and sparkles lustrously.

History has, for the most part, dealt kindly with America's creative giants, recording their innovations and accomplishments, rendering them the recognition and praise they richly merit. But history is a chronicle recorded by people, and people are merely fallible humans, so the chronicle is flawed. There are gaps in it, unaccountable omissions from the list of those who wielded an important influence over the shaping of the nation, unwarranted slightings of many of the country's significant innovators.

Largely overlooked, for instance, is Philip Mazzei, an Italian who settled in Virginia in 1773 to establish an experimental farm. However, it was not in farming practices but in a far different field that he bestowed on America a gift of supreme importance. Deeply committed to improving conditions for the common man by eliminating bigotry and repressive government, he wrote stirring articles and delivered ringing speeches urging the cause of independence. President John F. Kennedy observed two centuries later that the moving words of the Declaration of Independence—"All men are created equal"—can be traced to Mazzei.

Or consider Mary Engle Pennington, who in the late 1800s when it was still considered "unladylike" for a woman to enter the sciences, earned her doctorate as a chemist and then went on to contribute more than any other single individual to raising the nutritional level of the food that America eats. During a notable career that ended in 1952 when she was eighty, Dr. Pennington devised many of the techniques and health standards of the milk, egg, and poultry industries; she established methods for the safe storage and transportation of perishable foods, improved the design of home refrigerators, and helped develop the processes that resulted in creation of the modern frozen-foods industry.

And there was Emile Berliner, employed as a porter in a New York City laboratory, who became fascinated by physics and especially by electricity, embarked on experiments on his own after the laboratory's professional staff went home at night, and emerged as an inventive genius. In 1877, when twenty-six, he devised the microphone, and ten years later produced the flat phonograph record that replaced Edison's inferior cylinder. Then he designed the system of pressing records from a master disc, formulated the durable shellac to coat the copies, and went on to invent several key devices for use in the fields of aeronautics and acoustics. Yet who recalls his name today?

Or consider Dr. Joseph Leidy, one of the nation's outstanding and least heralded scientists. No other figure in nineteenth-century America surpassed him in the importance and wide variety of scientific gifts he bestowed on the nation. Among other things, he discovered the cause of trichinosis disease in humans, founded the science of parasitology in the United States, was the country's leading paleontologist and natural historian of his time, was a founder of the National Academy of Sciences, and clearly described the doctrine of evolution more than five years before Charles Darwin reached the same conclusions and published them in a study that gained him worldwide acclaim.

Then there was ten-year-old Uriah P. Levy, who ran away from home in 1802 to be a ship's cabin boy, rising to become captain of a schooner before he was twenty-one and giving it all up to enlist in the U.S. Navy as a noncommissioned sailing master when the War of 1812 commenced. A superb, courageous mariner, once again he rose from the ranks and was commissioned a lieutenant. Harassed by fellow officers who resented him both as a Jew and as a former enlisted man, he endured duels and six courts-martial on trumped-up charges to eventually become a commodore—then the Navy's highest rank—commanding the Mediterranean Squadron. During his forty-eight years in the Navy he led a ship's crew ashore in Mexico to halt a force of insurgents preying on resident Americans, declined an invitation from Dom Pedro to resign from U.S. service to accept an exalted post in the emperor's Brazilian navy, and was instrumental in bringing about much needed reforms in the U.S. Navy, notably the abolition of the cruel practice of flogging sailors for infractions. But Commodore Levy also preserved for the nation an irreplaceable portion of its heritage. In 1836, then a lieutenant, he was appalled to discover that Thomas Jefferson's magnificent Monticello estate had fallen into the hands of an eccentric farmer who had destroyed the grounds and gutted the buildings in a vain attempt to raise silkworms on the premises. Determined to halt this rape of a national treasure and this affront to the memory of the third President, Uriah Levy bought Monticello and, between tours of sea duty, devoted himself and his resources to restoring it as a gift to the American people.

Norbert Rillieux was a New Orleans black who invented the ingenious system of multiple-effect steam evaporators that revolutionized the sugar-refining industry in 1843 and then was adopted by other industries dependent upon large-scale, economical refining of products—and this method still is in use today.

When Margaret E. Knight died in 1914, she had been granted an astounding total of twenty-seven patents for inventions, ranging from a machine for making paper bags to a shoe-cutting machine to sleeve-valves for motors to improvements for the engines of automobiles.

These—and the scores of others who are shrouded in the dim recesses of the past—are the forgotten weavers of the American fabric. They are the unheralded and unsung who gave the nation so much of its vitality and strength, so much of its character and meaning. Shortchanged by history, they are America's neglected innovators. Some who have received far less than their due appear in the pages that follow. To all of them this book is dedicated, in gratitude and in admiration.

2
Men of Iron

THE TIME WAS 1643. THE PLACE WAS THE
banks of the Saugus River, a dozen miles north of
Boston. It is in that year and in that place that an
accounting of America's neglected innovators
ought logically to begin.

That section of land through which the Saugus
flowed seemed to possess little to warrant diverting
the attention of the leaders of the young, struggling
Massachusetts Bay Colony from the multitude of
problems confronting them. The riverbanks were
unattractive swamps, a desolate stretch of oozing
bogs and shallow, muddy ponds. On both sides of
the river heavily wooded pine forests swept down
to the swamps, but they did not dispel the dismal

atmosphere that overhung the area. However, in those dreary Saugus bogs the colonists had lately discovered an asset that excited their imagination: mixed in with the oozing mud was a substantial surface deposit of limonite. Many of their hopes for the future were linked to that clay-like ore scattered so thickly through the swamp.

The colonists knew that limonite had long been used in England for smelting into iron. In fact, the ore was popularly known in England as "bog-iron." The colonists also knew that huge amounts of charcoal would be needed for the smelting furnaces in which the ore could be transformed into usable iron. Girdling the swamps was that heavy growth of pines from which a steady supply of charcoal could be produced. So the Saugus claimed the attention of the colonists because it was the source of two of the inescapable requirements for making iron: the ore and the charcoal.

There was also a third, equally inescapable requirement that had to be satisfied before America could for the first time commence production of iron: someone with the skills and experience to build the furnaces and to operate them. But nowhere in the Massachusetts Bay Colony or in any of the neighboring colonies could such a man be found. Then in 1643 all that changed when John Winthrop, Jr., son of the governor of Massachusetts, went to England and recruited a group of ironworkers to return with him to the New World. Among that group was Joseph Jenks, a Welshman.

Jenks had not leaped at Winthrop's offer of employment in America; he had, in fact, been reluctant to accept it at all. At forty-one, he was not as deeply bitten by the bug of adventure as some of the younger workers gathered by Winthrop. And, unlike many of them, he was a married man with a family to care for and thus could not as readily move to distant shores. Furthermore, as a highly skilled master ironworker he was already well established where he was, respected for his talents, admired for the depth of his knowledge of all aspects of his craft. But the very factors that made him hesitate to join the group were the factors that made Winthrop want to lure him to America. The younger man kept urging, and finally Jenks accepted. Too cautious to burn his bridges behind him, he decided to leave his family at home until he had time to determine whether America was to his liking.

When he stood for the first time on the banks of the Saugus and looked about, Jenks realized the magnitude of the undertaking. There in a wilderness of swamp and forest a complete ironworks was to be built; yet none among the colonists really understood what such a complex project entailed. So much to do and so little to do it with, Jenks thought. He realized that as the senior and most experienced of the artisans Winthrop had recruited, his was necessarily the major responsibility for organizing and directing the entire enterprise.

So Jenks got to work as planner, draftsman, instructor, builder, problem solver and supervisor.

There were the furnaces themselves to design and build, the primary furnaces for smelting the ore into pig iron and several smaller furnaces—some for forming the pigs into bars, some for melting the pigs for casting in molds (which also had to be designed and built). This would be the heart of the undertaking, so Jenks begrudged any time he had to spend away from the creation of the furnaces. Nevertheless, he had to devote long hours to the bogs, studying the terrain and estimating the richness of the limonite deposits, marking off some sections for ditching and draining to make the ore accessible, designating other areas for dragging with scoops to snag the ore.

Meanwhile Jenks set teams of woodsmen to work felling trees and cutting the timber into proper lengths. Part of the logs he stacked in huge piles to fuel the furnaces. He turned the rest of the logs over to the charcoal makers to burn just to the point where the wood becomes transformed into charcoal. The charcoal would be an indispensable ingredient of his iron, and he knew that for every ton of ore he smelted, he might need as much as 125 bushels of it.

Ore in its natural state contains oxides that have been formed by interaction between it and the oxygen in its surroundings. To convert crude ore into usable metal, the oxide impurities must be removed from it in a process depending largely on the addition of carbon, of which charcoal is one form. What Jenks understood so well, and what local officials only dimly comprehended, was that melting ore in the furnace would accomplish nothing unless this complicated process worked properly.

Once the ore became sufficiently heated in the furnace, charcoal-carbon would have to be added to the molten mass in carefully controlled amounts. Then lime, obtained by crushing oyster shells, would have to be added to the mix. Next, streams of air created by leather bellows would have to be played over the molten ore. If the combination was right—the heat, air, lime, charcoal, and ore—a chemical reaction would cause carbon to combine with the oxide impurities to form carbon dioxide that would pass out of the furnace as waste gas.

Part of the carbon would remain in the processed metal, and the quantity remaining would determine the character of the iron. With just a trace of carbon, the iron would be soft and easily worked. With a carbon content of 2 percent, it would be much harder and more durable but still workable in a forge. With between 2 and 4 percent carbon, it would be too brittle for forging but would be suitable for casting in molds. Years of experience had developed in Jenks a sensitive understanding of all this and an intuitive ability to judge when the molten mass in the furnace had the proper carbon content to produce the kind of iron he wanted.

Jenks seemed to be everywhere and doing everything—sketching at the drafting table, surveying bogs and woods, building stockpiles of limonite, charcoal and lime, supervising construction, making tools that were otherwise not available, writing reports to the authorities. Like a jigsaw puzzle that is being solved, all the pieces began to fall into place. The Saugus ironworks was coming into being.

There was a festive holiday spirit when the furnaces were fired up for the first time. Members of the Massachusetts Assembly and townspeople from Boston rode out to witness the initial smelting as it got under way. In keeping with a long-standing tradition among ironworkers, the first product made from the first batch of ore smelted was a cast-iron cooking pot. Looking at that cooking pot, cast by his own hand in a mold he himself had made, in an ironworks that was to a great extent the result of his own ingenuity, resourcefulness and sweat, Jenks knew that he had now become a part of this new land. He sent for his family.

Jenks devoted himself energetically to operation of the ironworks, but adjacent to it he built his own forge as a private enterprise, having been granted that right by the grateful Assembly. So now a forge joined the country's first smelter, and Jenks worked a gruelling schedule to keep each running efficiently. Fortunately, his son—Joseph Jr.—was rapidly emerging as a talented ironworker, and more and more he found that he could safely leave routine operation of the forge to young Joseph.

If it is possible to pick out from the broad

expanse of America one single spot that deserves to be called the cradle of the nation's industrial might, it would be difficult to deny Saugus that honor. And it would be difficult to deny Jenks credit for being the father of American industry. Between them, Saugus and Jenks led the colonies on their first steps along the path toward industrialization.

Jenks was clearly the right man in the right place at the right time. Taking dozens of apprentices under his wing, he set about teaching them his skills, sharing with them his intimate knowledge of iron and its characteristics, creating in them a detailed understanding of the process that commences with crude ore and ends with a finished, useful iron object. After they had absorbed his patient teaching and had developed sufficient competence to venture out on their own, his students spread through the colonies to help create new forges and new furnaces. In turn, these new ironworks served as magnets for the establishment of other manufacturing enterprises that depended on reliable sources of iron and of ironworking craftsmen.

The simple truth is that making iron was more than a profession to Jenks; it was also a hobby, something to do for the sheer satisfaction and pleasure of the doing. When their day's work ended, other men might pick up their fowling pieces and go hunting, or they might slip down to the river to see if the fish were biting, or they might gather with friends for a companionable tankard of ale. But for Jenks work and pleasure were the same, so that he was always occupied with iron, always trying to make the metal perform new tricks or trying to make it perform old tricks in a new and better way. There was nothing about the metal or the things that were fabricated from it that he did not seek to improve. Thus, even the scythe—the oldest and most basic of tools formed from iron—did not escape his attention.

The ancients had used scythes for harvesting grains and grasses, and over the centuries it had remained just as it had been in the beginning—a short, thick, curved blade attached at an angle to a stubby wooden handle. Using the scythe was slow, tedious work because the thick blade had to be whacked through the grain instead of slicing its way through easily; and because the implement could only cover a narrow swath on each pass, it took many passes to cover a whole field. Jenks did what nobody before him had done—he redesigned the venerable but inefficient scythe to make it perform more effectively and more easily. Abandoning the traditional blade, he substituted one that was longer and thinner and would accept and hold a keen edge. To provide durability and prevent the reshaped blade from bending, he added an iron spine along the back of the blade. And to eliminate stooping, he lengthened the stubby handle. What Jenks ended up with was an implement that sliced neatly instead of hacking, and one that could be used for more effortless harvesting over a wider area. Recognizing the merit of the new design, the Massachusetts Assembly granted Jenks a patent on it; it was the first patent to be issued in the colonies.

Boston had by this time begun to grow into a fair-sized town. The municipal authorities, surveying their bustling community of wooden houses and shops, realized it was vulnerable to fire. To put themselves into position to cope with that threat, they turned to the innovative Joseph Jenks and asked him to create for them an "ingine" to fight fire. Responding to this challenge, the ironmaster designed and built the nation's first fire engine, a horse-drawn vehicle equipped with a huge water tank, a discharge pump, and a hose line.

In the Jenks family it was clearly a case of like father like son; the older man's expertise and devotion to his craft had rubbed off on Joseph Jr. Encouraging, explaining, demonstrating, the father kept polishing the son's skills, kept expanding his appreciation of what could be done with iron to make it serve a larger role.

The time came when Joseph Jr. was a master ironworker in his own right, restless to strike out for himself. The opportunity he had been seeking presented itself in 1671—a chance to buy sixty choice acres near the new settlement of Providence in Rhode Island.

No forge had yet been built in Providence nor, for that matter, anywhere else in that colony, and the need for one was obvious. But, beyond that, the site that Joseph had his eye on was along a river at a point only four miles from Providence where the riverbed dropped off steeply in a series of falls that could furnish an abundance of waterpower. Young Jenks recognized the potential of the location. He bought the site. Then he married the girl he had been courting, and the newlyweds set out for Rhode Island.

Jenks had inherited enough of his father's level-headedness to put first things first. He realized that his plans for developing the site had to commence with the practical matter of providing living quarters for his bride and himself. Together with a few artisans he hired, he hauled in supplies from Providence and built his house on a knoll overlooking the river; it wasn't grand, but it was weathertight and comfortable. With that behind him, he got busy on the forge, establishing it on the riverbank so that he could easily barge his iron wares downstream to Providence. Then he immediately built a sawmill where the surge of the water provided more than enough power for the machinery. His father had trained him well—his designs were sound, his construction true; the forge and the sawmill worked flawlessly.

The attractions of the location—its proximity to Providence, its navigable river, its abundant waterpower, all of the things that had drawn Jenks to the site—now became apparent to others. New settlers arrived. Soon gristmills were operating at the falls, and houses were scattered along the bank. The settlement grew large enough to need a name, and

Pawtucket—Indian for "falling waters"—was the choice.

In 1675, only four years after Jenks had built the house, the forge, and the sawmill that had become Pawtucket, everything lay in ruins. The entire community had been put to the torch by marauding Indians. The settlers, eluding the attackers and fleeing downriver to the protection of Providence, had been lucky to escape alive. For the next two years Jenks chafed restlessly in Providence as he waited for peace to be restored to the region. Then he and his wife returned to Pawtucket to begin all over again.

The ruins confronting them were a sad, disheartening sight. Between the pillaging of the Indians and the ravages of weather, little of value remained. Still, Jenks picked through the debris and was able to salvage a few odds and ends of equipment that were still usable. Then he set about rebuilding his forge, sawmill, and house. For good measure, he also built a bridge spanning the river so that the community could develop along both banks. And develop it did, steadily and solidly. Soon Pawtucket was no longer a diminutive settlement. It was now becoming transformed into a town. Because Jenks had led the way, had harnessed the waterpower at the falls, had created a forge to fabricate the iron needed for industrial growth, Pawtucket would in time emerge as a major manufacturing center.

Back in Saugus, meanwhile, an aging Joseph

Jenks, Sr., was stubbornly resisting the encumbrance of his mounting years. Still actively and enthusiastically operating America's first ironworks, he continued taking apprentices into his forge to teach them the ironworker's skills, continued devising new and better ways to use the metal to which he had devoted his lifetime. In 1683, at the age of eighty-one, he died. At the time of his death he had on his drawing board the plans for a plant to draw iron rods into wire.

The debt owed to Joseph Jenks—both the father and the son—is enormous; yet today the name of this innovative, pioneering pair has fallen through the cracks of history. To add melancholy insult to historical injury, surviving records do not even agree on the proper way to spell the family name—the few yellowing chronicles that still exist list it variously as Jenks, Jencks, or Jenckes.

3
Con Man with
a Touch of Genius

ABEL BUELL HAD A QUIRK IN HIS CHAR-
acter—he always kept a sharp eye out for a chance
to make a quick profit, and it did not upset him if he
had to venture onto the wrong side of the law to
take advantage of it. The plain truth of the matter is
that Buell was a con man at heart, a conniver, a
manipulator. But if he was a rascal who was often a
thorn in the side of the authorities, he was also a
talented, resourceful man of many skills. So the
authorities, pocketing their pride, often turned to
him for help in matters that suited his skills.

The Buell story commences in Killingworth,
Connecticut, where he was born in 1742. His
childhood was unremarkable; he got into his share

of mischief, but no more than did other youngsters. When he reached his teens, a local silversmith, Ebenezer Chittenden, agreed to take him on as an apprentice.

Learning the silversmith's craft in colonial America was a long, arduous trial. One first had to learn how to melt down silver coins in a crucible— the only source of working silver in those days— and how to cast the molten coins into ingots. Then one had to laboriously hammer out the ingots into sheets. Only after the apprentice had mastered these muscle-wearying preliminaries could he begin to learn the techniques of following patterns to cut the sheets of silver, soldering pieces together, forming rounded objects by carefully striking the silver with a mallet to force it against an iron die, making wire by drawing narrow strips of silver through the tapered holes of a "draw block," making molds for casting small objects like handles and ornaments, using the polishing anvils and polishing hammers, and engraving decorative designs.

Chittenden was a demanding taskmaster, but he was also a patient and thorough teacher, especially when he discovered that Buell had a natural talent for working the silver. Slowly, as the apprentice mastered the various aspects of silversmithing, Chittenden assigned him increasingly exacting operations to perform until eventually Buell was able to start out with a double handful of coins and end up with a gleaming array of attractive objects ranging from marrow spoons and snuff boxes to sugar bowls and teapots. He developed a special competence for engraving. Chittenden himself confessed that his young apprentice could outperform him with the burin, the pointed tool with which the engraver cuts into the surface of the silver to create his decorative design.

Self-confident and imbued with a spirit of independence, Buell was anxious to be his own boss. In 1762, though he was only twenty and Chittenden advised against it, he borrowed money with which to open a small silversmith's shop in Killingworth. Townspeople shook their heads and freely predicted that the impulsive youth would regret his hasty action. To everyone's surprise, Buell seemed to prosper almost from the very start of his venture into business for himself. He paid off the sums he had borrowed to buy his equipment, he outfitted himself with extravagantly expensive clothes, he got married, and he furnished a house for his bride, all in that order and in rapid succession.

Buell's affluence puzzled his neighbors because they seldom saw customers enter his little shop. Yet, despite his apparent lack of business, his purse always seemed to be full. Townspeople remarked to one another about this paradox, and they tried, unsuccessfully, to figure out the answer. While the town wondered how he was able to accomplish it, Buell continued to spend money with careless abandon.

In time, gossip about the young silversmith who

had found a way to flourish, though he had so few customers, reached the ears of the Connecticut authorities. They, too, were curious to discover how Buell managed to keep his purse so full. An official investigation revealed the secret. Buell, skillful engraver that he had become, was energetically devoting his sure, delicate touch to altering the design of five-shilling notes issued by the state of Connecticut, so that they emerged from his talented hand as five-pound notes. Buell was promptly arrested on a charge of counterfeiting currency.

In March, 1764, he was tried and convicted. His sentence was harsh by today's standards but was normal for those times: branding on the forehead with a "C" for counterfeiter, clipping of the left ear, imprisonment, and confiscation of all his property. As soon as the sentence was announced, his wife, humiliated and shamed, left town never to be seen again. Buell did not seem unduly disturbed by her disappearance.

In carrying out the sentence, the authorities—taking note of Buell's youth—decided to temper justice with mercy, so the brand was burned into his scalp above the hairline where it would not show, and instead of cutting a notch from his ear, it was merely nicked so that it would be scarcely noticeable.

Abandoned by his wife, disgraced and in jail, Buell nevertheless retained his buoyant spirit and a confident belief in his ability to improve his situation. He began his search for a way to ease his predicament by making himself useful to the prison officials, volunteering his skills to repair and maintain their tools and equipment and making trinkets for them. Pleased by their young prisoner's model deportment and grateful for his talented services, the officials responded by relaxing the rules, giving him free run of the workshops to use as he saw fit. This was a promising start, and Buell made the most of it. Utilizing scrap materials that were available, he set out to perfect an idea he had conceived for a lapidary machine, a device for cutting and polishing gemstones for jewelry. In this way and under these unlikely circumstances he invented and built an effective lapidary machine.

Buell's intuition led him to the conclusion that if he played his cards adroitly, his invention could turn out to be the key to unlock the prison gates for him. Very carefully, he cut and polished a crystal on his machine. Then, using all the skill he had acquired from Chittenden, he designed and made a beautiful silver ring in which he mounted the crystal. Then he sent the ring to the prosecutor who had appeared against him at his trial, accompanying his gift with a letter declaring that he had learned the error of his ways and wished for nothing more than the chance to return to society to make amends for his youthful transgressions. Then he sat back to await developments.

He had not long to wait. Whether it was the ring or the letter that did the trick is not clear and is really unimportant. What is important is that he got the kind of action he had been hoping for—the prosecutor promptly petitioned the Connecticut Assembly for his release. The legislators acted favorably on the petition. Having served less than six months behind bars, Buell was granted his freedom. But Buell was never one to content himself with half a loaf. He boldly requested the Assembly to restore his full civil rights, in effect to wipe out his criminal record. His request was granted.

Once he was again a free man with his full rights restored, Buell resumed silversmithing. But now he was well aware he would have to operate very circumspectly because everyone would be watchful for another misstep. The prospect held no great attraction for him. It was not that he no longer felt satisfaction in silversmithing and especially in the engraving that had been at the root of his earlier troubles; it was simply that a brashness and impudence in his character made him shy away from a life of quiet, dull respectability. So he worked the silver with something less than real enthusiasm while he looked around for opportunities that held the promise of more excitement.

He found what he was looking for when he discovered the plight of colonial printers, who were totally dependent upon European sources for type. Because the supply line was so long, so uncertain, and so expensive, printing type was scarce in America and printers guarded whatever type they possessed. Looking into the matter more closely, Buell learned that no type foundry existed in America to provide a domestic source of that vital commodity because the process demanded exacting skills that had not yet been developed in any of the colonies. To become America's first type founder —that prospect generated excitement in Buell. And with the self-confidence that never seemed to desert him, he was sure he could accomplish the feat.

Buell's work was cut out for him. Local printers could offer him little technical advice because their experience had been confined to how to use the type, not how to make it. So Buell had to rely on his instincts and on experimentation. First, he taught himself to use the sharp gravers, chisels, and files to shape a raised letter on the flat end of a steel punch, heating the steel to make it softer and more malleable so that it could be worked. His experience as an engraver helped him master the technique, but even so, it went slowly because an individual punch had to be made for each capital letter, each small letter, each punctuation mark, and each numeral.

Next, every punch had to be hammered just so against a separate square of copper with enough force to leave a clear, clean impression of its shape indented into the softer copper. Then the copper square bearing the impression—called a matrix— was fixed to the bottom of a mold into which molten metal—five parts of lead to one part of antimony—was poured. As the molten mixture cooled and hardened, it assumed the shape that had been impressed into the matrix. Now the shaped, hardened metal was lifted from the mold and examined for rough edges and imperfections, each of which had to be filed away carefully. This long, complicated process created only a single piece of usable type. To provide the type sufficient for printing just one page of a book might require as many as 2,500 such pieces of type.

Tenaciously, Buell mastered each aspect of the complex procedure and, applying himself determinedly to the overwhelmingly demanding task, completed an entire set of type. In 1769 a Boston printing firm, Edes and Gill, printed a page that had been set from beginning to end in type designed and cast by Buell, the first printing that had ever been done from type created in America. A surviving copy of that history-making page is preserved today in the Yale University Library.

Initially, the Connecticut Assembly had become aware of Buell five years earlier when he had taken it into his own hands—literally—to raise the value of the colony's currency. Now the Assembly was exposed to a new, praiseworthy dimension of his talents, and they were deeply impressed with it. Anxious to provide a domestic source of supply, the legislators asked him to establish a type foundry in New Haven, turning over to him the sum of 100 pounds as an aid in getting it started. Never the one to look a gift horse in the mouth, Buell expressed his thanks and pocketed the money. But he kept putting off a start on the project. It wasn't that he did not believe it was worthwhile, it was simply that he had accomplished what he had set out to do—he had created America's first type—and now the matter no longer held challenge and excitement for him. So while the legislators assumed that Buell was laying the groundwork for a commercial type foundry, he was, in fact, looking about for new fields to conquer.

What claimed his attention now was cartography —map-making—which was in distressingly poor shape in the New World. Throughout the colonies there was an acute need for reliable maps and charts—for bridge building and road construction, for navigating along the coast and through the inland waterways, for laying out the boundaries of political jurisdictions, for exploration and expansion, for agriculture, commerce, transportation and other purposes—yet vast areas of the colonies were either not mapped at all or had been poorly and inaccurately mapped.

There are two inter-related aspects to cartography. One is the on-the-ground survey of an area to measure and record distances, elevations, contours and natural formations of every type. The other is to take this mass of data and to transpose it into a precisely rendered copperplate engraving from which a map of the area can be reproduced. At every step of the way the opportunities for error are enormous. The surveyor can misread his instruments, misalign the reference points on which he bases his measurements, make a mistake in his computations. The engraver can misinterpret the surveyor's complicated data, or be inexact in his rendering of a topographic feature, or make an error in transposing a surveyor's measurement on the ground into a diminutive line on a copperplate. A map is such a severely scaled-down portrait of the actual area it represents that a mistake of only a fraction of an inch on the engraving can result in a blunder of many miles on the ground. It is not difficult to see why people in early America, where cartography was not yet an established profession, were harassed by the inadequacy of maps.

The basic technique for engraving copper is little different from that for engraving silver, so Buell, with his silversmithing experience, had little difficulty in transferring his skill from one metal to the other. But in engraving silver, the object was for the craftsman to give free rein to his imagination in order to create a pleasing, artistically satisfying design. In copperplate engraving for cartographic purposes, the craftsman had to hold his imagination in check; he had to be a disciplined, exacting artisan who was seeking to produce mathematical truth, not attractive art.

Once Buell set out to do something, he was never content to stop with a halfway effort. In order to become an accomplished cartographer, he plunged into study of the surveyor's techniques so that he could speak their language, understand their methods and their calculations, and appreciate their problems. He taught himself to use surveying instruments and to perform the related mathematical computations. Meanwhile, he practiced making copperplate engravings.

Although he was deeply committed to this effort to make a cartographer of himself, Buell could not ignore the practical realities of everyday living, so—to provide an income for himself—he opened a small silversmith's shop in New Haven. He devoted only enough time to the silversmithing to assure money to meet his living expenses; the rest of his time he devoted to map-making. Actually, that is not entirely accurate—the rest of his time he devoted to map-making *and* Aletta Devoe. He had always had an eye for the ladies, and they for him, finding him a lively companion with a quick wit and a gift for charming conversation. He and Aletta were married in 1771, and he wasted no time in teaching her the basic rudiments of his silversmith shop so that she could help out in it and thus free him to spend more time on his cartography.

In 1773 Buell made his first significant contribution as a map-maker. The existing charts of the Connecticut River had long been troublesome to navigators because they were inaccurate in portraying sandbars and other hazards to shipping. A surveyor, Abner Parker, had recently completed new soundings and measurements which corrected the inaccuracies of the past. Buell took Parker's data, substituted it for the flawed material, and engraved a copperplate for a new, reliable chart of the river entrance. Navigators entering the river could now breathe more freely.

Abel Buell's most notable cartographic accomplishment was to come years later, just after the signing of the 1783 Treaty of Paris that ended the Revolutionary War and marked the formal birth of the United States of America. Within months of the treaty signing, a large map—41 by 46 inches—was published in New York, depicting all of the agreed-upon territories of the new United States. This was the first map of the emergent nation to be compiled and engraved by an American: Abel Buell. But that milestone in map-making lay in the future. For the present his most pressing concern was to stay out of jail.

The Connecticut legislators had not forgotten that they had granted Buell 100 pounds to aid him in establishing a type foundry, and from time to time they had been badgering him to begin showing some concrete progress in the undertaking. Now it was clear that they had lost patience with his dillydallying and were about to take action against him on charges of fraud. To compound his difficulties, he was also being threatened by James Rivington, a printer who was reproducing maps from engravings made by Buell. Many months earlier Buell had borrowed money from Rivington and had repeatedly delayed repayment. Angered, the printer was threatening to haul him into court, where he would risk sentence to debtor's prison.

Doubly vulnerable to ending up on the wrong side of a prison wall, either as a fraud or as a debtor, Buell decided that the time had come to put some distance between himself and both Rivington and Connecticut. It was a decision in which loyal, loving Aletta fully supported him.

In 1775 Abel Buell discreetly disappeared from New Haven. To all questions concerning her husband's whereabouts Aletta blandly replied that she had not the slightest inkling, but she did insist forcefully that his debts would be paid. Working hard to squeeze a profit from the shop, she managed over the next two years to restore to the Connecticut authorities the 100 pounds they had previously granted to Buell. In the meantime, the Rivington problem had evaporated. Rivington, a Tory who was violently opposed to American independence, had joined the British army in New York at the outbreak of the Revolution. Having cast his lot with the enemy, he was no longer able to sue Buell in the American courts.

In 1778, after it had become apparent that the Connecticut legislators, having been repaid, no longer had any interest in prosecuting him, and after Rivington had conveniently removed himself as a threat, Abel Buell turned up once again in New Haven, much to Aletta's undisguised joy. Unfortunately, her joy was of short duration—before the year was over, she became sick and died.

Buell resumed his silversmithing and his cartography and, to everyone's surprise, he even established the long-promised and long-delayed type foundry. He missed Aletta and he thought of her often and fondly. However, he met Mrs. Rebecca Townsend, a buxom widow, and she began to fill the void Aletta's death had left. In 1779 he and Rebecca were married.

Poor Rebecca! She might as well have remained a widow, she saw so little of her new husband—he was much too busy to take time out to play the role of bridegroom. Anyway, this was the third time around for him, and the novelty of marriage had worn thin. In a burst of activity, Buell had now embarked on a bewildering variety of new ventures in addition to his smithing, engraving, and type casting. Several of these new undertakings were purely commercial in nature—operating a line of packet boats between New York and New England ports, conducting an auction house, exhibiting side-show freaks, and investing in a marble quarry. None of these strangely assorted pursuits prospered for very long, although some did manage to limp along for some years.

Buell was much more successful when he devoted himself to activities that depended upon his skillful, sensitive hands and upon his ability to understand complex technical details. In 1783 he invented a corn-planting machine, and two years later he invented a machine for coining money. The Connecticut authorities promptly awarded him a three-year contract to mint copper coins for them. He must surely have taken great delight in the odd twist of fate that had led Connecticut to jail him for counterfeiting its currency when he was twenty and then, twenty-three years later, had led the state to contract with him to mint its coins.

For the next dozen years Buell's life was a ferment of activity as he turned from one to the other of his diverse interests. He cast type for numerous printers throughout Connecticut and farther afield, made important cartographic engravings, silversmithed, improved his coining machine, and fashioned handsome jewelry, cutting and polishing stones for much of it on the lapidary machine he had invented in jail so many years earlier.

Responding to the urging of engineers seeking his help, he drew detailed plans for many of their projects and constructed beautifully precise working models of their complex machines. With it all, he continued experimenting with several inventions of his own devising and tried to keep a watchful eye on his many faltering business projects. Buell was so driven by the demands of his multiple activities and by the ideas for new endeavors that kept popping into his fertile imagination that he had not noted that Rebecca was quietly fading away; he was surprised when she died in her sleep one night.

In 1795, embarking on yet another undertaking, Abel Buell built a cotton mill in New Haven. The mill was hailed as a triumph of technical efficiency, but Buell had little talent for supervising the commercial side of the operation. In any event, with all of the other claims on his time, he could devote only scant attention to the mill. It, like his other businesses, began to wither. Never losing his characteristic optimism nor slowing his frantic pace, Buell did what he had done so often in the past—he married again and he cast about for fresh challenges.

By 1799 all of his commercial enterprises had failed. At last he faced up reluctantly to the inescapable fact that he was simply not cut out for the role of a businessman. He moved to Hartford to concentrate on things at which he excelled: silversmithing and engraving. However, still unable to resist the lure of taking on at least one new project, he also began practicing the craft of armorer. Soon he was fashioning handsome pistols that were much admired.

At last a measure of order and of routine had been introduced into Abel Buell's life. He was pleased with the work he was turning out, pleased that his creative skills were as keen as ever. The less agitated pace of his activities was commencing to feel comfortable to him and he also discovered that, for the first time ever, he was finding joy in leading a more normal sort of life. Then, quite suddenly in 1803, his fourth wife died. The pattern of life that he had begun to grow so content with was broken and he could not restore it. He lingered on in Hartford for another two years before moving on once again, this time to Stockbridge, Massachusetts, where he practiced silversmithing and produced some of the most beautiful objects of his long career in that craft.

Around 1813 Buell was swept up in the religious revivalism that was then in vogue in New England. He had never before taken much interest in religion, but now he embraced it with all of the enthusiasm that he had always previously lavished on any of the undertakings that had claimed his attention. He attended every prayer meeting he heard of, urged everyone he met to follow the word of the Bible, condemned liquor and all forms of immorality, and declared his repentance for all his past escapades. Ironically, he was by now quite bald, so that the branded "C" once hidden above his hairline was plainly visible to his listeners as he urged morality on them.

Age was rapidly catching up with Abel Buell. His mind remained active, still bubbling with ideas, but now there was a nagging stiffness in those marvelously skilled hands that had given America its first type and its first national map, that had created a lapidary machine and a corn planter and a coining machine, that had fashioned silver teapots and jewelry and engravings and pistols and engineer's models. Frustrated, he found that he could do less and less, until finally he could only sit, his once magic hands resting idle in his lap.

In 1820, penniless and alone, Abel Buell returned to New Haven and was admitted to the Alms House. Two years later, at the age of eighty, he died and was buried in a pauper's grave.

4
The Man Who Invented Mass Production

THE GAME HE AND THE BLACKSMITH'S apprentice had devised turned out to be so much fun that as soon as Joseph Evans returned home he described it in detail to his brother, Oliver. He explained how, during the blacksmith's absence, he and his friend had poured water into a musket barrel, trapping the liquid inside the cylinder by squeezing wadding into the barrel opening to form a tight seal. Then they had placed the water-filled musket barrel so that one end of it rested on the edge of the smithy's fire. Within moments there was a clap of noise like a firecracker as the wadding shot from the end of the barrel, propelled into the air on a cloud of steam.

Joseph was excited over the loud pop that he and his friend had been able to create, but Oliver was more impressed by the power of the steam. If steam could develop enough force to shoot wadding into the air, he reasoned that it ought to be possible to figure out ways to get that force to perform other, more useful tasks than simply making a noise like a firecracker. That is the way Oliver Evans' mind always worked. Others might be content with a bang simply for the sake of the bang itself, but he would always wonder about the whys and hows of it and, above all, whether there might be some way to extract a benefit from it.

Oliver Evans was born in 1755 on a farm along the Christina River near Wilmington, Delaware. His father, a bootmaker by training, had turned to farming only a few years earlier, and so far his most successful crop had been children—a dozen in all, with Oliver arriving at the midway point in the succession. Under the circumstances, with so many children to raise and with free public education not yet in vogue in Delaware, Oliver was lucky his father was able to send him to school long enough to get a solid foundation in the academic basics. His formal education came to an end when he reached fourteen, and arrangements were made to place him into apprenticeship with a wheelwright and wagon-maker.

The man with whom Oliver was placed, while stern and demanding, knew his trade and taught it conscientiously. The youngster was pleased with the arrangement because he enjoyed working with his hands as well as his mind. So by day he learned the skills of a wheelwright and wagon-maker and by night read whatever books he could borrow. The books he sought most avidly were those dealing with the sciences and technology, which in those days was known as the "mechanick arts." Few technical books were available, so he prized those he was able to borrow, studying and restudying them carefully.

One book made a deeper, more lasting impression on him than the others. It contained a description of an English device called a Newcomen engine. Immediately Oliver was reminded of the game his brother had played with a water-filled musket barrel, for this was an engine that depended on steam to operate. A massive affair, the heart of the Newcomen engine was a hollow metal cylinder six feet high and one foot in diameter. It held a movable piston connected to a long arm that extended out through the top of the cylinder. The arm was counterbalanced in such a way that when it was in its normal position it held the piston at the top of the cylinder. The cylinder was closed at the bottom except for two valves, one connected to a pipe leading to a large steam boiler, the second connected to a source of cold water.

With the piston in its normal, upraised position the steam valve was opened, permitting steam to surge from the boiler into the cylinder, where it quickly displaced and expelled the air that was present. Then the steam inlet was closed and the water valve was opened, releasing a spray of cold water over the interior of the cylinder. The cold spray caused the steam to condense, creating an instant vacuum that sucked the piston down to the bottom of the cylinder. Then the weight of the counterbalancing arm took effect, raising the piston back to its normal position at the top of the cylinder; air once again filled the interior. Now the steam valve was re-opened and the whole cycle was repeated. The rising and falling of the piston was used to power machinery, most often mine pumps. If the Newcomen engine was working well, and if the valve tender knew his business and could maintain the proper rhythm in opening and closing the valves, it could develop as much as five horsepower.

Evans, fascinated by the engine, remembered the lesson of the musket barrel. The musket had demonstrated that steam had a power and strength of its own, yet the Newcomen engine did not take advantage of that strength. Instead, it used the steam only as a means of creating a vacuum. He could not escape the conviction that this was a roundabout and inefficient way to make use of the steam, that it would be more effective to employ the steam as a direct driving force.

By this time Evans was approaching the end of his apprenticeship, a period when he had matured mentally as well as physically. His voracious appetite for science books and the thoroughness with which he digested their contents had given him a broad, even sophisticated understanding of technical matters, so he saw other ways in which he felt the engine could be altered to improve its performance. Feeling it was presumptuous to think that he—so young and so inexperienced—could hope to improve upon the work of established engineers, he nevertheless believed he could. While he speculated about steam engines, more pressing matters claimed his attention.

Relations between the colonies and England had been steadily worsening, causing shortages of manufactured imports. Thinking about these shortages, Evans was struck by the fact that lack of even a relatively simple device could cause widespread hardship. Textile mills and home spinners alike were severely hampered by the shortage of "cards," used in pairs to comb out the tangled mass of raw wool as the initial step in the spinning process. The cards—leather paddles containing rows of curved iron teeth—were needed in enormous quantities. To try to fill the great void left when English manufacturers halted their shipments, women and children in America were laboriously cutting leather into paddles and piercing the tough leather with sharp awls to make the series of holes into which the teeth would have to be inserted. It was tedious, difficult work. But the next step was worse—snipping thin iron rods into the tooth-length segments, forcing each segment into its hole in the paddle and crimping it into place firmly, then bending each tooth into the proper curve for combing out the wool effectively. Despite the enormous time and effort that were devoted to the undertaking, the output of cards was unable to keep up with the need.

When an accident kept Evans at home for several weeks, he used the time to try to figure out a way to overcome the card problem. Since the teeth seemed to be the key factor, he turned to them first. Analyzing the way in which each tooth was individually cut to the right length and then bent to the proper shape by hand, he realized that this was an operation requiring the kind of repetition and precision better suited to a mechanical device than a human hand—if such a device could be invented. Using his imagination and knowledge of the "mechanick arts," he set out to invent it.

After conceiving and discarding several approaches as impractical, Evans succeeded in developing a concept that he believed would work. He drew sketches of the design and showed them to his family and friends. The device would, when cranked by the operator, cut iron rods into tooth lengths, then automatically bend each tooth to the proper shape for carding wool. Everyone was skeptical. He persuaded a blacksmith to build the machine from his drawings only after dosing the man with enough rum to wear down his resistance.

The machine worked exactly as Evans had promised it would. He asked for and was granted a chance to demonstrate it before the Delaware

Legislature. Impressed, the lawmakers praised the machine but rejected Evans' request for $500 to establish a plant to manufacture it. A Wilmington businessman who had witnessed the demonstration asked Evans to sell him the manufacturing rights, offering an initial payment of $200 and promising additional payments after production began. Evans agreed. Then he designed an additional machine that pierced the leather paddles and inserted the teeth into them automatically, turning out 300 finished cards per day.

Between them, the two machines provided the means of overcoming the card shortage in the colonies, but all the young inventor ever received for his breakthrough was the $200. Not only did the Wilmington manufacturer default on his agreement, other factories promptly pirated the inventions and began exploiting them with neither payment nor credit to Evans. There is one account of a Boston pirate firm that turned out 150,000 cards annually on machines copied from the Evans originals.

Usually Oliver Evans was gentle and even-tempered, with a pleasant, courteous way of speaking, but when he believed himself wronged, he erupted in anger. This was one of those times. He roared with outrage over the theft of his inventions, especially since there was nothing he could do about it; there was not yet an enforceable system of patent protection. But very soon a more momentous event claimed center stage: the outbreak of the Revolutionary War.

Along with two of his brothers, Evans enlisted in a Pennsylvania militia company and marched off to an encampment near Philadelphia. He never became involved in combat, and in 1778 he and his brothers returned home. There had always been a special bond of closeness between Oliver and his brother Joseph. Hearing of a general store for sale in Tuckahoe, Maryland, they agreed to become partners in its purchase. It was a sound venture, doing a steady if unspectacular sale of farm equipment, household utensils, hardware and other necessities.

For miles in every direction from Tuckahoe there was a patchwork of small family farms, almost all growing wheat as the major crop. A network of streams cut through the region, and it was the rare stream that did not have at least one mill on its banks to grind the wheat into flour. Roaming through the countryside, Oliver Evans was appalled by the inefficiency and crudeness of the mills.

When wheat arrived at the mill, the miller and his assistants had to heave the sacks onto their shoulders and then climb a stairway to the top of the granary, where they emptied their sacks and then retraced their steps to the ground for another load. From the top of the granary the wheat had to be fed by hand into a hopper, from which it dropped between the waterpowered millstones to be ground into meal. The ground meal dropped from the stones into a large wooden trough, from which workmen shoveled it into tubs. As the tubs became full, they were hoisted to a loft, where they were dumped out and their contents raked into piles to cool off and lose moisture. Once the meal had cooled and dried, it had to be shoveled up once more, this time onto a chute, down which it slid to the bolting hopper. There workmen screened the meal to separate bran, dirt, and debris from the flour. It was an enormously cumbersome, wasteful process that turned out dirt-speckled flour of uneven quality.

The more familiar Evans became with the mills around Tuckahoe, the more convinced he was that the millers were going about it all wrong. They saw their job simply as a number of separate start-and-stop, back-breaking operations. Evans looked at milling through different eyes. He could visualize it as a *system* instead of a number of separate operations—as a comprehensive, coordinated method that substituted machine power for manpower.

Encouraged by Joseph, to whom he explained his concept, Evans began to wrestle with the problem, breaking it down into segments and then defining the purpose of each segment and analyzing the way the miller went about achieving that objective. He looked for the strengths and weaknesses in everything the miller did, but especially for the weaknesses. Then he considered every alternative way he could imagine to perform each of the operations, carefully analyzing them for flaws and their adaptability into a single coordinated system. Slowly he began to evolve several ideas that he felt merited further evaluation and analysis.

Evans married Sarah Tomlinson, daughter of

a Delaware farmer, in 1783. As time passed, his stack of engineering drawings and technical notes gradually grew. He worked steadily and single-mindedly toward his goal of designing a totally new kind of mill. In 1785 he was ready to put his concept to the test. With Joseph as his partner, he undertook construction of a model mill on a plot of ground they owned jointly on Red Clay Creek, near the farm where he had been born. He knew exactly how he wanted to proceed, had planned each step down to the minutest detail, so the construction moved smoothly and rapidly. When the mill was completed that fall, it was unique— the world's first automated mill, the forerunner of the kind of technology that would later become the keystone of the age of mass production.

In the Evans mill, the arriving grain was hoisted directly from the delivery wagons to the top of the mill by an automatic bucket elevator. As it was discharged from the elevator, the grain passed through a machine where a fan blew across it to free it of debris. Next, the grain was fed mechanically to the grindstones that crushed it into meal, after which another set of bucket elevators carried it to the upper floor, where a revolving rake spread it out mechanically to cool and dry. From the drying floor the meal was conveyed by an endless belt to a bolting machine that sifted it to separate the bran from the flour. The flour then passed into barrels by gravity-feed; the barrels were sealed; and the automated circuit of the mill was at an end.

The mill was a remarkable achievement, a major

industrial breakthrough. By introducing a coordinated system of endless-belt bucket elevators, lateral conveyor belts, and screw-feed tubes, it provided automated movement throughout the mill, both vertically and horizontally. Cleaning, raking, drying and sifting, previously hand operations, were now accomplished by Oliver Evans' machines. In order to power all of these conveyor devices and machine operations, the mill incorporated an ingenious system of pulleys and gears so that the same waterpower that turned the grindstones did double-duty by powering everything else in the mill. Thus, the entire operation could be handled by a single individual and would consistently turn out a clean, high-grade flour with far less wheat lost during the manufacturing process than in traditional mills.

The curious came from miles away to see the Evans mill. A number of farmers began bringing their wheat to the mill for processing, but Oliver Evans had no wish to settle down into the life of a miller. What he wanted to do was to sell his technology to others so that they could duplicate his new kind of mill. He had secured from both the Delaware and the Pennsylvania authorities "monopoly rights" granting him the privilege of charging a fee for the use of his systems and machine designs. He thought, naively as it turned out, that the evidence of his model mill would be sufficient to bring millers flocking to him for licenses. When the millers—set in their ways and suspicious of radical change—clung obstinately to their old, clumsy methods, he felt frustrated. Arming Joseph with drawings and descriptions of his mill, he sent his brother on a sales tour through the two states that lasted for months but did not result in the sale of a single license.

In 1790, when the United States patent law came into effect, Evans secured a national patent on his mill. (It was the third U.S. patent issued. The first was for a process for producing potash; the second was for a candle-making device.) As soon as his U.S. patent was issued, Evans appointed sales agents to offer use permits throughout the country at $40 each. His agents succeeded in selling only a very few. Despite slim sales, more and more of the Evans mills began to operate in various parts of the country. The trouble was that millers were simply pirating his invention without buying permits, just as his wool card machines had been pirated years earlier. Evans was livid with rage. He brought suit against pirates left and right, but even winning a suit was almost profitless after lawyers' fees had been deducted. In 1791 President Washington observed one of the few Evans mills that had been legitimately licensed and was so favorably impressed by it that he purchased a permit himself and installed the system in his mill at Mount Vernon.

Evans' innovative perceptions and engineering talents had made his mill a resounding technological success. Making it a financial success would clearly be a quite different matter. Wisely, he left day-to-day handling of the financial problems to the sales agents and the lawyers so that he could turn his attention to an interest that he had held in check for many years: the steam engine. He had never lost his fascination for the engine, and now he intended to do something about it. In 1793 he moved to Philadelphia, then the capital of the United States. It seemed a likely place to watch the efforts of his agents and lawyers and come to grips with the steam engine.

In the quarter-century that had elasped since the awkward, inefficient Newcomen engine had appeared, a number of inventors had introduced changes and improvements into the basic design. James Watt in England had been particularly successful in creating a much-improved engine.

Examining Watt's engine, studying its specifications intently, Evans could appreciate the innovations that the Englishman had engineered into it. One was immediately familiar to him because he himself had envisioned it years earlier when he had studied Newcomen's design—using steam to thrust directly against the piston rather than indirectly by creating a vacuum to move the piston. He admired the engine and all of its improvements, but he felt that the design was not without flaws. The major shortcoming he perceived was that, despite its very considerable size, Watt's engine produced relatively little power.

It seemed to Evans that the most logical way to increase the power output would be to introduce steam into the cylinder under high pressure. In

Watt's engine, steam was under pressure of four or five pounds per square inch, but Evans visualized an engine in which the steam would be under pressure of 25 to 30 pounds per square inch. He reasoned that an almost tenfold increase in steam pressure would not only create a much more powerful piston stroke but would also permit a reduction in the bulk of the engine, thus giving it the important plus of portability. However, he recognized the risk in working with high-pressure steam, clearly seeing the need to find effective ways to strengthen the engine, and especially the boiler, so that they would not burst under the increased pressure.

Evans settled down in his workshop to perfect a safe and efficient high-pressure steam engine. Because he was so thorough in his approach to the undertaking, so unwilling to jump to conclusions, his progress was necessarily slow.

From time to time he was diverted by business matters and law suits related to his mill patent, and by family matters. By now he had several children. He took delight in all of them, sometimes breaking off an experiment to play a game with them or to build them a clever toy. He was even diverted by other inventive ideas that came to him—thus, even while he was working on his engine, he managed to obtain patents for an improved method of manufacturing millstones, for a new type of stove, and for furnace grates. But his abiding preoccupation was the engine.

In 1801 his design concept was completed. He

built his first test model, a small engine. Though the cylinder was only 6 inches in diameter and the piston had a stroke of just 18 inches, this was no toy. Operating flawlessly, Evans' high-pressure engine had a remarkable power output. Putting his little engine to a practical application, he used it to grind gypsum, a mineral widely used as a fertilizer and as an ingredient for cement. The engine performed with complete reliability, grinding a half-ton of gypsum per hour in sustained use.

Having demonstrated the undeniable soundness of his concept, for which he was granted a patent, Evans immediately set about improving the basic design, for he firmly believed that nothing was ever so good that it could not be made a bit better. Then he built larger models that could be used for a variety of applications. He was not long in finding a use for his bigger, better high-pressure engines. Philadelphia municipal authorities, alarmed at the mountain of muck and refuse that had accumulated along the city's waterfront, had tried to dig their wharves free, trying to accomplish the task with hand-operated scoops mounted on a barge. They had had only minimal success. Now Evans proposed that he build a steam-powered dredge to do the job; the city fathers, skeptical but becoming desperate, agreed to pay Evans $3,000 if his dredge could dig the waterfront out of the muck.

Knowing exactly how he wanted to proceed, Evans moved ahead confidently. As soon as his design sketches and engineering drawings were completed, he assembled a crew and built a sturdy flat-bottomed boat, 30 feet from its squared-off bow to its squared-off stern and 12 feet across, christening it *Orukter Amphibolos,* fractured Greek for "amphibious digger." He mounted the high-pressure engine and the steam boiler amid-ships, woodpile for fuel stacked close at hand. Digging was to be accomplished by an endless belt of buckets that let down into the water to scoop up the mud. At the stern was a paddle wheel to propel the craft. A clever system of gears and drive belts linked the paddle wheel and the continuous chain of buckets to the engine so that both were powered by the same source.

Obviously, no craft as unusual as *Orukter Amphibolos* could fail to attract attention, and there was always a throng of spectators in attendance as the dredge took shape. The onlookers nudged one another, smirking over their realization of a key fact that the inventor seemed to have overlooked: the construction site was more than a mile inland from the bank of the Schuylkill River. They could hardly wait for Evans to finally wake up to the fact that his boat was landlocked.

The gloating turned out to be premature. When all was in readiness, the inventor mounted his boat on two pairs of strong wheels and linked them to the drive belt that was intended to power the paddle wheel. Firing up his boiler, he waited for it to develop a head of steam. When he had built up sufficient pressure, Evans fed steam into his engine and engaged the gears. Creaking and clanking on its huge iron wheels, streaming a plume of smoke behind, the fifteen-ton vehicle took off exactly as the inventor had expected it to.

When he reached Center Square on Market Street, Evans could not resist the temptation—he grandly circled the Square several times, treated astonished townspeople to the sight of the first wheeled vehicle ever to move on an American road under its own power. Then he drove *Orukter Amphibolos* down a slope and into the Schuylkill at low tide. As the incoming tide raised the water level, it floated the craft free of its temporary land wheels, and Evans re-attached the drive belt to the paddle wheel in the stern. He engaged the gears; the paddle wheel turned; and *Orukter Amphibolos* steamed out into the river, now treating spectators to a view of the world's first amphibious vehicle. Later, when Evans had demonstrated that the dredge could perform the job the city had contracted for—removal of the mud and debris clogging the waterfront—the municipal authorities paid him his $3,000.

In 1808, receiving a Congressional extension of his flour mill patent, Evans redoubled his long-standing efforts to secure payment from the millers who had been infringing his patent rights. He exploded with righteous indignation the following year when a judge, hearing an infringement case involving a different inventor, ruled that the granting of patents was not in the public interest and that

60

therefore the public had the right of free and unrestricted access to anything patented. Storming through his workshop and his home, he snatched up the sketches and technical notes of all of the projects he was working on. Throwing all of his papers into the crackling fireplace, he told his startled wife that he was destroying them to remove temptation from any of his children or grandchildren to follow "the same road to ruin that had subjected me to insult, to abuse and robbery all my life." A few months later the judge's absurd ruling was reversed by a higher court and the rights of patent holders were reaffirmed. But even before the reversal, a more subdued Evans had admitted to himself that when he threw his notes and drawings into the fireplace, he had simply gotten carried away by his anger. The fact was that he could no more stop inventing than he could stop breathing. So now he had to devote the next several months to trying to reconstruct from memory as many as possible of the papers he had fed to the flames.

A demand had developed for the Evans high-pressure steam engine. To satisfy it, over the next half-dozen years he built and installed more than twenty-five of them in various types of manufacturing plants in several parts of the country. His largest model, a 100-horsepower engine, was the pride of the Philadelphia waterworks.

In 1816 his wife died. The inventor was now sixty-one, but looked and felt older. He was plagued by a liver ailment and rheumatism, and his eyesight was failing. Nevertheless, he continued with his engines, his lawsuits, and with visualizing innovative concepts in his fertile imagination. Among his concepts, a quarter of a century before it was finally developed and patented by someone else, was the basic principle of the mechanical refrigerator.

After a brief illness, Oliver Evans died in 1819. As he was being buried, an editor, commenting on the several remarkable contributions of the inventor, wrote in his newspaper: "Few men have been as useful to society as Oliver Evans. . . . His contemporaries never appreciated him at his true value; but an understanding posterity will place his name among those who are most truly distinguished for their eminent services rendered to their country and to humanity."

The editor's prediction that future generations would hail Oliver Evans, granting him his full due for his brilliant accomplishments, turned out to be ill-founded. A better indication of how the future would deal with him came in 1822, three years after his death, when the last patent infringement case he had submitted to the courts finally came to trial. The verdict was rendered against Oliver Evans.

5
The Ice King

IF FREDERIC TUDOR HAD RUN TRUE TO form, he would have become a staunch pillar of New England society, leading the life of a cultured, dignified gentleman with a taste for fine wines and a gift for charming conversation. But Frederic Tudor was a maverick, a free spirit much too impulsive and self-willed to do the expected. All his life he would be an original—an impatient, outspoken nonconformist, supremely confident in his ability to attain whatever goals he set for himself. His fiery bent would lead him in new and strange directions. But after he had blazed the trail, multitudes would follow in his path.

The Tudors were one of the truly distinguished

families in the Boston of the Revolutionary era. They were on intimate terms with most of the notables of the new nation and with many of the visiting dignitaries from abroad, and entertained them frequently. Frederic's father had practiced law with John Adams after graduating from Harvard, and then had accepted a temporary commission from George Washington to serve him as the first judge advocate general of the American Army. His mother, well educated and cosmopolitan, was noted for the grace and generosity of her hospitality. The children—two boys older than Frederic, who was born in 1783, two girls, and a boy younger—were brought up in an atmosphere of sophistication and self-assurance that rubbed off on them at an early age. It was taken for granted in Boston that the girls would marry well when they reached marriageable age and that the boys would follow in their father's footsteps, attending Harvard and then either practicing law or entering government service. But Boston hadn't reckoned on Frederic Tudor.

The first indication that Frederic was a maverick came when he was thirteen, and it came with a boldness that would be typical of everything he did in later years. Taking advantage of his parents' absence on an extended tour of Europe, he told the master of the school he attended that he would no longer be coming to school. Then he obtained a place for himself as an apprentice clerk with Ducosten & Marshall, a leading mercantile company. When his parents returned and discovered what had happened, they were stunned. They tried their best to persuade their headstrong son to return to school, but he could not be budged, insisting that a business house would be the best schoolroom for him because it was in the world of business that he had decided to make his future.

Frederic kept a sharp eye on everything that went on at Ducosten & Marshall, constantly studying the firm's operations and trying to absorb the fine points of the extensive commercial transactions his employers conducted both domestically and abroad. Delighted with the zeal and attentiveness of their young clerk, his supervisors encouraged his interest and made a special effort to teach him all that they could.

By the time he was fifteen, Frederic decided he was ready to attempt a commercial venture on his own. Saying nothing to anyone, he quietly entered into correspondence with a Cuban broker, who had no idea that he was dealing with a boy. Having saved a small sum of money, Frederic commissioned the broker to buy a modest quantity of Havana cigars for his account and to ship them to Boston. When the cigars arrived, he disposed of them at a profit and immediately ordered a second shipment. Over the months that followed, he continued his quiet little forays into foreign trade, dealing now in molasses as well as cigars.

It was clear that Frederic Tudor looked on his employment at Ducosten & Marshall as only a temporary resting place as he prepared himself for an upward march toward bigger and better things. But to give him his due, he was diligent and energetic in discharging his responsibilities to his employers, even though they had no place in the future he had in mind. When he was eighteen, by now well versed in the techniques of trade, he left the firm and set himself up as an independent trader, using a borrowed desk in the office of a family friend. Relying completely on his own ability to judge the trend of future supply and demand, he embarked on commercial ventures in whatever commodities seemed to him to offer opportunities for profit: tea, flour, nutmeg, cotton, sugar, wine, candles, pimento. His judgment was sound more often than not, so his transactions brought him a comfortable income.

Fascinated by the world of commerce, excited by the high degree of risk that was an inherent part of each venture, he was restless with nervous energy, his mind forever occupied with the complexities of his dealings. Yet, he was not all work and no play. He found the time to become one of the livelier members of Boston's young set, amusing at parties, enthusiastic about attending the theater or frolicking on a picnic.

It was in mid-1805, just a few weeks short of his twenty-second birthday, that Frederic Tudor's life was radically altered by an idle conversation at an engagement party for one of his sisters. The talk drifted into a discussion of a custom then gaining considerable popularity among the more affluent local families: the cutting of ice from frozen lakes in wintertime to store for summertime use. The Tudors themselves had recently dug their own icehouse on some lakeside property they owned on the Newburyport Turnpike. One of the group observed, more in jest than seriousness, that there ought to be a profit for anyone who harvested local ice and then figured out a way to ship it south for sale in the hot Caribbean islands.

To the others it was simply an outlandish, amusing idea, something to smile over and quickly forget. But not to Frederic Tudor. He was seized by the idea, stimulated by its originality. Especially appealing to him was the possibility he could perceive in it for great gain. To take something that nature made available free and to convert it into a commercial commodity of value was something to stir his imagination.

Studying the map of the Caribbean region, he saw at once that Cuba, the largest and most densely populated of the islands, would be the most promising market. But before tackling Cuba, he wanted to test the feasibility of the concept, so he chose Martinique as the target for an initial shipment of ice. Located 2,000 miles from Boston, it was more distant than Cuba, so would provide a properly gruelling test. He at once dispatched two agents to Martinique to find and rent a suitable structure to serve as a storage depot for the ice and to stir up local interest in his intended shipment.

Next, he searched the waterfront for a vessel to haul his ice southward. Ultimately, he found and purchased the brig *Favorite*. She was a small but swift two-masted vessel. Her hull was sound and, at $4,750, the cost was within range of his pocketbook.

Now all Tudor needed was the ice to load aboard his ship. For that he had no choice but to wait for nature to get to work on his behalf. Restlessly, he welcomed each chill breeze that blew to herald the approach of winter. Finally, after a few false starts, a hard freeze set in and turned Fresh Pond, just north of Boston, into a thick sheet of ice. Gathering together a work crew, Tudor started them chopping blocks from the lake. In mid-February 1806, when the *Favorite's* hold was laden with ice, he sailed her toward Martinique.

In early March, almost all of its cargo of ice still intact, the *Favorite* reached Saint-Pierre, then Martinique's port and main town. There Tudor found with dismay that his agents had failed him and disappeared. Realizing that only a few local people who had traveled abroad had ever seen ice, Tudor arranged with a printer to hurriedly print and distribute handbills announcing *Favorite's* arrival with ice and describing in detail the uses and benefits of the frozen delight. The townspeople, doubtful about the unfamiliar product, adopted a wait-and-see attitude. Tudor, checking on the situation below-deck, was alarmed to find that melting was commencing to accelerate in the sustained heat. Knowing he needed a quick, dramatic way to break through the wall of resistance he was encountering, he set out for the town's most popular restaurant, the Tivoli.

Turning on his considerable charm, Tudor invited the Tivoli's proprietor to make history in Martinique by being the first to serve ice cream. The proprietor listened politely but insisted that the ice would turn to water before it had done its job. Tudor drew himself erect, and in a commanding tone that overrode the restaurant-keeper's objections, ordered him to have cream, sugar, and flavorings in readiness in the morning, when he would return with ice and himself make the ice cream.

The next morning Tudor returned with fifty pounds of ice. As he had promised, he froze the cream, packing it in buckets of ice to keep it from melting. Word raced through Saint-Pierre that ice cream was available at the Tivoli, and the proprietor quickly sold out, chalking up a tidy profit of $300. All smiles and apologies, he went to the brig to get a fresh supply of ice. Others followed in his wake to do likewise. Tudor sighed with relief, for the melting of his cargo was now becoming worrisome. His undertaking had come dangerously close to being a total failure.

It was early summer when Tudor returned to Boston. He had been able to salvage something from the Martinique experience. His total investment had been $10,000, and his return had been only $6,000, but the difference was offset by the value of the *Favorite*. And he had proved to his satisfaction that ice could be transported over long distances to hot-weather ports. More important, he had learned that the key to success would be the establishment of proper facilities to preserve the ice once it reached its destination. He saw this as a need for two different types of facilities: a depot to store and sell the ice ashore, and special chests in the homes of purchasers to hold the ice and provide storage space for foods to be cooled by it. He set out to design both types of facilities.

Family icehouses in New England were customarily built below ground level, but Tudor believed an above-ground structure would be more practical for use abroad. He began experimenting with buildings of different sizes and shapes, and with walls of various thicknesses, trying to come up with an ideal combination. He also experimented with the use of sheepskin as an insulating material. In addition, he conceived of his icehouse as a building made of interlocking panels so that it could be shipped to its destination in sections that could be taken ashore to be fitted together easily and snugly. At the same time, for home use, he designed ice chests with tin-lined compartments for ice and with space for food storage, hiring carpenters to build models of the chests, which he called "ice refrigerators."

In early December, 1807, his experimental models having shown considerable promise, Tudor deemed the moment ripe for tackling Cuba. This time he left for Havana to attend to the preliminaries himself. Soon after he landed, word reached Cuba that President Jefferson had placed an embargo on all American shipping because the Napoleonic Wars, then raging between France and England, was threatening the security of neutral vessels on the high seas. This put a stop to Tudor's ice trade in Cuba before it had started. There was nothing for him to do but return home. He found more bad news awaiting him when he arrived there.

Tudor's father and several other prominent men had joined together in a land-development investment that had started off on a promising note but then had suffered a series of reverses from which it could not recover. His father had lost everything and was left with debts he could not pay. Despite his record of honorable service to the nation, he was threatened with debtor's prison under the harsh laws then in effect. Outraged by this affront to his father and to the family's good name, Tudor used all of his available funds and borrowed more wherever he could to pay off the most pressing of his father's debts, pledging to discharge the rest of the obligations as soon as he could. Thus he saved his father from the humiliation of jail, but now the debts—and the threat of prison if they should not be paid—were his.

Temporarily restrained from international trade by the embargo, Tudor turned to other avenues in pursuit of income. For years his family had owned a small farm near Boston, regarding it as a place for vacations rather than a business; now he worked hard to turn the farm into a paying proposition. Unfortunately, with his characteristic rashness, he used most of the farm's profits to finance an unsuccessful search for coal deposits on an island off the Massachusetts coast.

Even while farming and looking for coal, Tudor continued work on designs for newer and better icehouses. He was anxious to return to the ice trade because he was more convinced than ever that it held the potential for making him rich. He was also spurred on by the fact that others had now swung around to his view and were also seeking to enter the ice trade. In 1810, the shipping embargo having been lifted, he borrowed funds and embarked for Havana for a fresh attempt to capture the Cuban market.

As soon as Tudor reached Cuba, he called on the local authorities. Employing great diplomacy, he obtained an exclusive six-year license to sell ice in Havana. Thus he stole a march on would-be competitors, squeezing them out of that market for at least six years.

Tudor at once hired carpenters to build an icehouse incorporating the latest design he had conceived. Once construction was well under way, he hurried north to secure a shipment of ice. By year's end, sales in Havana totaled $7,500. Leaving a manager to operate the depot, Tudor returned to the United States to initiate new business ventures.

Within a few months he had expanded his ice operations into Jamaica, installing as his representative on that Caribbean island his younger brother.

At last everything seemed to be moving ahead smoothly. But it was only the calm before fresh storms. The first new blow was struck in Cuba. Sales there had been gaining strength throughout the year, and for all of 1811 they totaled $9,000. However, because of—in Frederic Tudor's own words—"the villainous conduct" of his Havana agent, only $1,000 ever reached Boston. Sales in Jamaica were only modestly successful, and brought Tudor only a dribble of money. So he still had money problems. Deeply in debt, he was constantly pressed by impatient creditors.

In March 1812, one of the creditors obtained a warrant against him. He was arrested and placed in a debtor's cell in Boston. Mortified and indignant, after a few days Tudor managed to raise enough money to obtain his release. In June, he received a fresh setback when war broke out between the United States and England and he was forced to suspend shipments of ice to the Caribbean.

Restricted in his activities by the constraints of the War of 1812, he could do little more than concentrate on the farm and plan for the future. In June 1814, one of his creditors took legal action against him and he was once again lodged in jail for a night.

In December the war came to an end, and Tudor

immediately made plans to reopen his ice depot in Cuba. He had designed an improved icehouse to be built in sections in Boston and then shipped to Havana for final assembly.

His problem was, as usual, money to finance the undertaking. It is a tribute to his powers of persuasion that he was able after several weeks of effort to raise sufficient funds to hire carpenters to build the sections of his icehouse.

When he arrived in Havana in 1815, Tudor found a suitable site on the waterfront and put a crew to work erecting his building. The structure was square, two stories high, with two sets of thick walls—the inner wall separated from the outer wall by an air space. The only entrance to the building was by way of an outside stairway leading to the second floor, where the sales office was located. A trapdoor on the second floor opened into the lower floor, which had storage space for 150 tons of ice. Erection of the building was completed in time to receive the first shipment of ice in March.

The icehouse design proved to be highly effective, keeping melting to a minimum. In the remaining nine months of 1815, sales totaled $10,000. With the Cuban operation now on firm footing, Tudor envisioned creating a vast network that would transport his ice to nations all around the world. Such an audacious undertaking would require tremendous capital investment. He could not find the money. But he did succeed in raising enough to expand into Charleston, South Carolina, and Savannah, Georgia, building a storage depot in each of those southern ports. Now, however, others were also shipping ice to those cities, so the competition was keen.

The rivals vying for the ice trade in Charleston and Savannah slashed their prices as each tried to lure customers from the others. The result was that profits were razor-thin. Tudor had one advantage over all of his competitors—he had his well-designed, efficient storage depots, while his rivals had no icehouses at all; they sold their ice directly from their ships tied up at the wharves. Shrewdly playing his competitors' game with more devastating effect than they, Tudor made his ice a penny a pound lower, no matter how low they cut their prices. All the customers came to him, while his rivals' ice turned to water in the holds of their vessels. As soon as the competition had melted away—literally—he raised his prices to a more rewarding level.

Business was a long cycle of ups and downs for Tudor—nicely profitable when his rivals were not in port, much less so when they sailed in and set off price-cutting wars. It was a three-year struggle before he was able to consolidate his hold on the market and to discourage the hit-and-run tactics of the competition.

Tudor was ready now to move into the largest city in the south, New Orleans. Again he was plagued by money. The heavy expenses of his current operations and the need to pay off old debts had prevented him from setting aside sums for major new undertakings, so once again he had to seek fresh loans. By this time he had a solid reputation as a man who eventually paid his debts in full and as a man who was successfully pioneering ice as a valuable commercial commodity. The most persuasive factor, perhaps, was that he was willing to pay the extravagantly high interest rates the moneylenders often asked—in one instance he had paid an astronomical interest of 40 percent. So creditors loaned him the money he needed to establish operations in New Orleans.

Ice was now becoming very big business. In 1820, Tudor's shipments to his depots in Savannah, Charleston, New Orleans, and Havana came to 2,000 tons—and still there was demand for more. Keeping pace with this demand was starting to cause considerable concern. If the winter turned out to be warmer than usual, the ponds around Boston would not remain frozen long enough to produce sufficient ice to meet the continually enlarging requirements. To compensate for these whims of nature, Tudor built a huge ice-storage warehouse so that he could draw from its stocks when mild winters prevented the ponds from filling his needs. There was also another growing problem—the requirement for a way to harvest ice from the ponds on a larger scale and more rapidly than ever before. To accomplish this he and a talented employee, Nathaniel Wyeth, pioneered a new method of harvesting ice.

Their system used a heavy steel device with two parallel, saw-toothed cutting bars mounted 24 inches apart. Drawn by a horse, the device cut deep grooves into the frozen surface of the pond. After a number of parallel grooves had been cut, the horse-drawn device was moved so that now it was cutting grooves that were at right angles to the first set. In this way a section of the frozen surface was cut into a checkerboard of two-foot squares. Next, crow-bars were inserted into the grooves, and each square was pried free of its neighbors. Then the separate squares were floated along a channel to shore, where they were lifted by a horse-powered elevator to a platform from which they were permitted to slide down a chute that deposited them into the icehouse. It was a rapid, practical system, producing blocks that could be stacked efficiently because they were all of uniform size.

As insurance, Tudor also built a standby icehouse on the shores of the Kennebec River in Maine. This foresighted move proved its value when the winter of 1827–28 turned unusually warm and lakes as far north as mid-Massachusetts did not freeze solidly. Cities up and down the eastern seaboard clamored for ice. Even Philadelphia, normally able to provide its own ice from local bodies of water, sought 7,000 tons. Tudor, using his facilities in Maine in addition to his huge Boston storage warehouse, dispatched shipload after ship-load of ice southward.

Those who a quarter-century earlier had scoffed

now referred to Frederic Tudor, respectfully and enviously, as the Ice King. It was quite true; he had become the undisputed king of the ice trade. But ice was not his only interest. He had never ceased embarking on whatever undertakings struck his fancy.

His most offbeat venture came in 1830 when the Massachusetts legislature was debating a bill for establishment of the state's first railroad. Convinced that railroads were bound to succeed, he tried to encourage passage of the legislation. He did this by the highly unorthodox and dramatic expedient of building a demonstration line at his own expense to generate enthusiasm for the pending bill. In his typical maverick fashion, he created a railroad unlike any in existence. He laid narrow-gauge track through several blocks of Nahant, a suburban Boston town where he had bought a house, then imported from Charleston a miniature steam engine of only one-half horsepower together with a tiny car that had seating capacity for only a single passenger. Crowds lined the streets of Nahant to watch the pint-sized train chug along at its top speed of four miles an hour, the engineer crouched at the tiny engine's controls as he hauled his solitary passenger in the attached car. The publicity generated by this ploy helped to get the bill passed.

In 1833 Tudor met Euphemia Fenno, an attractive New Yorker visiting Boston. She was only nineteen and he was fifty, but despite the disparity in their ages, they fell in love. They were married January 2, 1834. The middle-aged bridegroom should have been able to relax and to commence enjoying the considerable wealth he had finally succeeded in accumulating. But his luck ran out again. He had been speculating heavily and profitably in coffee, when, without warning, the bottom dropped out of the coffee market and left him with thousands of pounds of beans he could not sell. By mid-year his losses were approaching the two-hundred-thousand-dollar mark.

Typically, Tudor decided that the way to pay off his coffee debt was to borrow money to finance his long-planned expansion of his ice trade to more distant corners of the globe. Forming a partnership with two men of substantial means, he boldly planned the establishment of an ice depot in Calcutta, India. As soon as preliminary arrangements were completed, he carefully loaded a cargo of ice aboard the *Tuscany* and dispatched the ship. This time, skeptics said, he had overreached himself; the ship would reach Calcutta with nothing but warm water in its hold. Tudor was, as usual, supremely confident. After all, he was more knowledgeable about ice than any other man in America and more capable of loading and insulating a vessel in such a way as to preserve a cargo of ice to the maximum extent possible.

One lesson Tudor learned during his years of seeking the best way to preserve ice during long voyages was that it was not enough to line the vessel's hold with insulating material as a barrier to outside heat. It was also necessary to pack insulation into all crevices between blocks of ice to eliminate air channels, however slender, that could serve as passageways for warmer perimeter temperatures to penetrate into the ice mass. Earlier he had experimented with sheepskin as the insulating material. Then he had tried hay. Later he had turned to sawdust and had found it to be a superior, more workable insulator than either sheepskin or hay. It became his standard insulating material for ocean shipments and securing adequate, reliable supplies of sawdust became one of his concerns. When the Maine lumbering industry commenced in the early 1830s to make sawdust available in great quantity on a continuous basis he was relieved of his worries from that quarter.

Not until the beginning of 1835 did word finally reach Boston that the *Tuscany*, its cargo intact, had safely reached Calcutta, where its ice had created a sensation. Tudor's detractors were astonished by the feat, for the voyage to Calcutta had required four months and had crossed the equator twice. Now that the feasibility of shipping ice to the far side of the world had been demonstrated so dramatically, others rushed in to copy Tudor. A booming ice trade between the United States and Asia rapidly came into being.

This sudden creation of a valuable Yankee export commodity could not have come at a better moment for New England, for the region's economy was faltering badly. Tudor and his ice gave New England a brand-new export that was in demand in the Far East, and launched a widespread revival of trade with the Asiatic ports. Ice revived New England.

At long last, having for decades endured ridicule and disheartening reverses, Tudor had realized his goal of turning a Yankee liability—its freezing winters—into a golden asset. From Havana to Calcutta, from Rio de Janeiro to Singapore, his ice was playing a role in commercial establishments, hospitals, and homes. This enormous expansion of his network had required tremendous capital investment so that, while he was making more money than ever, he was also more deeply in debt than ever. This time, though, the bankers were urging him to borrow from them because it was clear to them that all of the Ice King's troubles were behind him. In 1849, when he was sixty-five, he paid off the last of his debts and was finally what he had set out to be: a very wealthy man.

But wealth did not greatly alter Frederic Tudor or his lifestyle. He still worked as industriously as ever, still sought new markets and improved methods of harvesting and shipping ice, still ventured at the drop of a hat into whatever undertaking captured his fancy. Year by year, his ice empire continued to flourish. In 1856 he dispatched a remarkable total of 363 shiploads of ice to 53 different ports in the United States, the Caribbean, the East Indies, China, Australia, and the Philippines. In London, when the new Persian ambassador met the American ambassador, his first words were an expression of his country's gratitude for the New England ice that was arriving in Persia regularly.

Throughout his life Frederic Tudor had been a man who thought original thoughts and then had the boldness and the drive to act on them. He gave one final bit of evidence of this in 1860, when he had reached the venerable age of seventy-six. He built Maolis Gardens in Nahant. Maolis Gardens was America's first amusement park. Thus, this notable and unconventional man even planted the seed that was to blossom into today's Disneylands. Four years later, the Ice King was dead. He had been actively planning new ventures until the very end.

6
The Gentle Giant

OBED HUSSEY WAS A BEAR OF A MAN—
solid, muscular, broad through the shoulders and
chest. His mouth formed a thin-lipped slash between his high cheekbones and his squared-off,
jutting jaw. A black eye patch, suspended from a
narrow band encircling his forehead, hung down to
mask his sightless left eye, the result of an accident
he had suffered in his early years. Obed Hussey
looked strong, rough, tough, even—with his black
eye patch—piratical. All in all, he seemed the sort
of man you would instinctively shy away from if
you met him late at night along a deserted pathway.

Appearances were deceiving. Hussey was, in
fact, quite the opposite of what he seemed to be. He

was a very gentle man, soft-spoken, unfailingly polite, sensitive, well-read, retiring, and shy.

Born in Maine in 1792, he was raised in Nantucket, Massachusetts, where his Quaker family moved when he was a young boy. Nantucket, as the nineteenth century was dawning, was a youngster's delight—exciting, vibrant, pulsating with the sights and the sounds and the smells of ships and boatyards, of sail lofts and ropeworks, of oakum and sperm oil. This was the golden age of the American whaling fleet, and Nantucket Island, off the Cape Cod coast, was the most important of all of the whaling ports.

Every Nantucket boy listened wide-eyed to the tales spun by the whalers, to their yarns about far-off places with strange names. And every Nantucket boy dreamed of putting to sea with the whaling fleet. In this respect, Obed Hussey was no different from other youngsters. In his mid-teens he went to sea.

It was everything the sailors along the waterfront had said it would be: exciting, exotic, thrilling. But for gentle, sensitive Hussey it was also something else that the sailors had not talked about: butchery.

When the lookout's shouted "she blows!" announced the sighting of whales, the crewmen hastily put over the side into their flimsy smallboats to pursue the animals—the hunt was on. Oars biting powerfully into the foaming water, the smallboats raced toward their quarry, each boat targeting a different animal. As soon as the straining oarsmen brought their boat within range of their prey, the harpooner in the bow let fly with his steel-barbed harpoon, sinking it deep into the giant whale. Enraged and in pain, the whale sometimes turned and fought his attackers, occasionally crushing the boat and spilling the sailors into the sea. But usually the tormented beast, trying to rid itself of the barb deep within its body, swam away frantically, towing the boat behind him. This was the storied "Nantucket sleigh ride," and it lasted until the tiring animal slowed enough so that the whalers could gain on him by hauling in on the line trailing back from the shank of the harpoon. When they were close enough, the sailors finished off the suffering beast with steel-tipped poles as it thrashed in anguish. It was slaughter on the high seas.

But there were always long periods during the voyage when the vessel simply sailed the sea, and these were the times that Hussey liked best. With the rest of the crew, he kept busy repairing gear, maintaining the ship's equipment and machinery, mending lines, scrubbing decks. When there was no more work to be done, he followed the whaler's traditional hobby—scrimshaw—the carving of intricate scenes in pieces of whalebone. He enjoyed using tools, handling them skillfully, and he found fascination in all of the mechanical devices aboard the ship. He examined each piece of equipment carefully to understand how it functioned. Learning how to keep the equipment in good running order gave him satisfaction. It was only when the whales were sighted and the blood began to flow again that the pleasure went from the sea.

When Hussey's vessel returned to Nantucket almost three years after it had set out from that port, he signed off as a crew member; he had had his fill of whaling. But he brought ashore with him something that had been shaped during those long months aboard ship: an abiding interest in mechanical devices.

Now Hussey commenced a period of wandering. A man of simple wants, he was able to satisfy them adequately by taking on odd jobs repairing broken-down equipment for farmers and shopkeepers. It was a happy time for him. He felt affection for the machines he worked on, appreciated the ingenuity with which they had been designed and built. Tinkering with them to determine what had gone wrong and then putting it right gave him a deep sense of satisfaction. Hussey could stand and quietly admire a machine the way a horseman admires a fine animal or an artist a great painting. Like them, he could appreciate the strengths, the coherent qualities of the object of attention.

Sometimes when Hussey watched someone at work—a farmer, artisan, shopkeeper, housewife —he wondered if it might be possible to create a device to perform mechanically some of the tasks that they pursued so laboriously by hand. He would mull the question for days, trying to discern ways in which it might be possible to do it.

Hussey's creative speculation and his persistent

tinkering began to bear fruit. He invented a machine for grinding corn and corncobs, another for husking the corn. He devised a machine for crushing sugar cane, designed an improved candle mold, and created an apparatus for forming hooks and eyes. These were all useful and practical inventions, but in matters related to himself Hussey was impractical. He was impatient with the business side of his inventions, more interested in their creation than in their exploitation for profit. So he left it to others to find what profit they could in his inventions, while he turned his attentions to other projects that captured his imagination and challenged his skills.

In the late 1820s, Hussey's wanderings eventually brought him to Baltimore, where he met Richard B. Chenoweth, a farm-implement manufacturer. As a dealer in agricultural equipment, Chenoweth had come across Hussey's devices for processing corn, so the man and his work were not entirely unknown to him. Now, in long conversations with the gentle, one-eyed ex-whaler, he realized that Hussey had a deep-seated urge to continue creating contrivances that could serve a useful purpose, and that he had the talent and insight to make success attainable. Chenoweth had an unused room in his factory; he invited the inventor to take it over as a workshop to test out his ideas. Grateful for this unexpected kindness, Hussey established himself in the factory, fitting out his room with workbenches and tools.

It is not clear whether it was Chenoweth or one

of Chenoweth's friends who proposed that Hussey try to invent a mechanical reaper for grain. It was a sound idea. The nation had been expanding westward at a rapid pace; enormous farms had been carved out in the fertile plains stretching westward from the Alleghenies. Harvesting the bounty of those vast croplands was a prodigious task; it was especially true of the huge wheatfields. All the wheat in a given area ripened at the same time, rather than gradually, as with most crops. Once ripened, the wheat had to be reaped quickly. In poor weather wheat had to be harvested within four days. Even if the weather were perfect, harvesting had to be completed in no more than eight days—or else the grain fell from the plants and nothing remained to be gathered. So when the wheat ripened, farmers and their families and whatever labor they could hire immediately took their scythes into the huge field and remained there day and night in a back-breaking race against time and weather.

Hussey knew little about farming, but he could readily understand how vital it was to have an effective, mechanical reaper to reduce dependence on hand labor and to speed the operation. Such a machine, he realized, would revolutionize agriculture.

Having found his supreme challenge, Hussey thought of little else. Throughout 1830 and most of 1831 he scarcely left his workshop during long working days. When he did emerge, it was only briefly to discuss technical matters with Chenoweth or some of Chenoweth's trusted employees. Totally immersed in his project, caught up in the complexities of it, Hussey often missed meals. Frequently he worked through the entire night, with only an occasional catnap at his workbench when he could no longer fight off fatigue.

As the months passed, Chenoweth and the factory staff became increasingly impatient to see what was taking shape behind the closed doors of the workshop, but they had to contain their curiosity. Hussey would let none of them enter, not even Chenoweth. Gently but firmly, he explained that he did not want to disappoint them with an unfinished and ungainly device that was still plagued with a multitude of unsolved problems.

It was late 1831 before Hussey was prepared to unveil his first crude model. Some years later Chenoweth's daughter, Sarah, who was present on that day, described what took place.

"When finally the model was completed," she wrote, "it was brought out into the yard of the factory for trial. This trial was made on a board, drilled with holes, and stuck full of rye straws. I helped put those very straws in place. Mr. Hussey, with repressed excitement, stood watching, and when he saw the perfect success of his invention, he hastened to his room, too moved and agitated to speak. A workman said that Mr. Hussey did not wish us to see the tears in his eyes."

What Sarah Chenoweth did not realize as she

witnessed the test was that she had seen nothing more than a simple demonstration that the ungainly device, when wheeled across a board that was stuck with straws, was able to chop through those straws automatically by pushing them against a sharp cutting-bar. It was an indication that the inventor was on the right track, that his basic concept was sound, nothing more than that. The girl could not appreciate that clipping straws stuck in a board was a far cry from harvesting huge fields thick with crops as far as the eye could see. A machine to cope with those fields had yet to be produced.

Hussey understood all this. He could draw encouragement and assurance from the start he had made, but he was not deluded by it. He knew it for what it was—the first step on the journey toward a reaper capable of harvesting actual crops in actual fields effectively and reliably over a sustained period of time. He took his crude model and once more disappeared behind the closed doors of his workshop. With that model as a guide, he began the complex task of designing the refinements and adaptations that would transform it from a factory-yard curiosity into a full-fledged farm machine able to master America's wheatfields.

As he laid out patterns, cut gears and sprockets, honed cutting-bars, experimented with variations in the design of each of the reaper's components, and analyzed the pros and cons of alternative methods of assembly, Hussey was unaware that on a Virginia farm scarcely 200 miles away from his Baltimore shop someone else was also trying to perfect a reaper.

The Virginia project had been initiated years earlier by Robert McCormick, a well-to-do farmer, miller, and distiller. McCormick, who had a keen eye for an opportunity for profit, foresaw that whoever could produce a reliable reaper would be creating a financial bonanza for himself. With money as his powerful incentive, he had set out to design such a machine on his farm in Walnut Grove in Virginia's Shenandoah Valley.

McCormick was not being unrealistic in thinking that he might be able to design a harvester. He had shown that he had a knack with mechanical contrivances. Already he had invented a threshing machine and had designed an improved system of bellows for the blacksmith's shop on his farm. However, the reaper was to prove too great a challenge for him. He produced a clumsy contraption, and no amount of tinkering and readjusting would prevent it from mangling crops into a tangled, unusable mess. He worked on it intermittently for years, but was never able to correct its glaring deficiencies. Ultimately—by coincidence it was in 1831, the same year that Hussey produced his first crude model in Baltimore—he admitted defeat and gave up the project.

McCormick's twenty-two-year-old son, Cyrus —aggressive, assertive, and self-confident—had inherited his father's flair for machines and his father's eye for profit. If his father was willing to call it quits on the reaper, he was not; so he picked up where his father had left off. Thus, two men were in the throes of inventing the reaper in 1831, one in Virginia and the other in Baltimore.

By 1833, Hussey had completely redesigned and refined his original model, which was now a vastly different machine incorporating a number of major innovations. No longer was it operated by pushing. Instead, it was now horse-drawn and was offset to one side so that the blades would pass directly over the rows of wheat. This arrangement prevented the horses from trampling the wheat in the path of the harvester.

But the most significant change was Hussey's invention of a radically new type of cutting-bar. It consisted of a long, sawlike blade whose leading edge was notched into sharp, triangular teeth. The blade was supported between a double row of metal fingers that stuck out ahead of it. As the reaper advanced through a field, the blade slid back and forth between the upper and lower rows of fingers. The fingers themselves caused the wheat the machine was passing through to divide into separate tufts. As the tufts were drawn against the cutting-bar by the forward progress of the harvester, the side-to-side, reciprocating motion of the blade caused its sharp teeth to slice through them. The cut wheat was then automatically deposited on a platform at the rear of the machine, where it could be raked together into sheaves. Power for the knife-blade and for the arm that deposited the cut wheat on the rear platform was provided by a crankshaft geared to the wheels of the vehicle so that the horses pulling it were performing double duty.

It was an ingenious system. The reaper's reciprocating knife-blade was a breakthrough that would later be adopted by many other inventors for a variety of cutting devices. Satisfied that he had at last created an effective reaper, Hussey applied for and was granted a U.S. patent on his invention in the summer of 1833.

Chenoweth, lavish in his praise and mindful of its tremendous importance to agriculture, insisted that the inventor must place it into commercial production. Hussey allowed himself to be persuaded. To find a market for his machine, he undertook to demonstrate the device in the field for farmers in the hope that once having seen it in operation they would place orders with him. So the whaler-turned-inventor hitched a horse to his reaper and took to the road with it. He was surprised that the reception from the farmers for whom he demonstrated it was only lukewarm. They saw that the machine did what Hussey said it would, but they were reluctant to start using a newfangled contraption so foreign to their experience. Hussey, no salesman, was too shy and reserved to try to wear down their resistance. Making his way westward, he finally obtained a few orders in Ohio and established a small factory in Cincinnati to manufacture them.

Meanwhile, back at Walnut Grove, Cyrus

McCormick was proceeding with his version of the reaper. In 1834, he built and obtained a patent on a model similar to the one Hussey had patented a year earlier. The chief difference was that its cutting-bar was stationary. (He was later to replace it with a reciprocating, saw-toothed cutter resembling the superior Hussey cutter.) For the time being, McCormick was so fully occupied with other business affairs that he postponed commercial production of his reaper.

In Cincinnati, Hussey produced the few harvesters for which he had obtained orders, but he was having a hard time making additional sales. An issue of the *Farmer's Register* in 1836 carried a very favorable account of the Hussey reaper, reporting that its "performance may justly be denominated perfect as it cuts every spear of grain, collects it in bunches of the proper size for sheaves, and lays it straight and even on the binders."

Had he been an aggressive businessman, Hussey might have capitalized on this unsolicited, highly complimentary publicity, but he allowed the opportunity to slip by. Then, to his surprise, on a trip through the East he received orders for a half-dozen reapers from farmers in Maryland. Heartened by this, he decided to concentrate on the East, where he felt more at home, and he moved his factory from Cincinnati to Baltimore. This would later prove to be a fatal error.

Soon after Hussey made his move to Baltimore, McCormick extricated himself from his other business interests so that he could devote himself to the commercial exploitation of his reaper. He improved his cutting-bar, redesigning it along lines similar to Hussey's. (Later Hussey was to sue him for patent infringement.) Then he set up a plant at the Walnut Grove farm to manufacture the reaper. Canvassing energetically for customers, he managed to create a limited market for his machine.

By that time, of course, Hussey and McCormick were well aware of each other's activities and were clearly established as rivals, each confident that his was the superior reaper. McCormick, who had a streak of showmanship in his makeup, issued a public challenge to Hussey to enter a field trial pitting one reaper against the other. Hussey accepted, and the two machines were tested side by side on a farm near Richmond. They turned out to be so evenly matched that the results were inconclusive. Further tests followed on other farms scattered through Virginia, but the results were also a stand-off. However, the tests did serve to whet interest in mechanical harvesting. Reluctance to buy the machines began to crumble. Each year the rivals were managing to sell a few more machines than in the previous year. This kind of slow growth held no attraction for McCormick. He would not be content to become a moderately successful manufacturer—he was intent on becoming an industrial giant.

Sizing up the situation astutely, he concluded that there would be little future in remaining in the

East to battle with Hussey for the limited market provided by the small eastern farms. He recognized that the real market for mechanical harvesters lay in the Midwest, where the huge farms were located. So he shifted his operation west to Chicago. It proved a wise move.

Whatever reaper developments McCormick did or did not invent is a matter of dispute. What is not in dispute is that he invented highly effective techniques for selling the reapers. Imaginatively and aggressively, never relaxing in his drive to generate more and more sales, he introduced business procedures into his Chicago plant that are taken for granted today but were revolutionary then. His innovations included market research, an installment payment plan for buyers, a mail-order department for replacement parts, advertising campaigns, a written guarantee with each reaper, a network of regional warehouses to assure rapid deliveries to customers. Stimulated by his enterprising techniques, the business expanded significantly and quickly. In a relatively short time he was well on his way to becoming the industrial giant he had sought to be.

Other manufacturers, looking at McCormick, were eager to be as successful. Several tried to get a toehold in the richly rewarding midwestern market by coming in with reapers of their own. McCormick sent in platoons of salesmen to out-hustle them wherever they tried to set up shop, so that they were stopped before they could really get started. Or he simply bought them out and closed down their operations. He was especially quick to buy them out if their reapers embodied any refinements that he thought could be usefully applied to his own machines.

While Cyrus McCormick was flourishing in the Midwest, Obed Hussey was withering in the East. He had made the fatal mistake of leaving Cincinnati to return to Baltimore. He realized that now, but still he clung stubbornly to the East, even though it had become abundantly clear that the prime markets were those in the Midwest which he had abandoned to McCormick.

In 1851 Prince Albert of England, who certainly could have bought any harvester he wished, ordered two Hussey machines for use on the royal estates. Cyrus McCormick would have known how to exploit this windfall of international recognition, but Hussey was not a promoter or merchandiser. He was pleased that Prince Albert had singled out the Hussey reaper for purchase, but he did not use it as a lever to increase his sales.

A number of years earlier, Hussey had brought suit against McCormick for patent infringement. The suit had dragged on, bogged down in the courts. Now, at long last, in 1859, the court rendered its decision—Obed Hussey won his case. Although the court had vindicated Hussey, the victory had come too late to do him any good. He had won the battle, but McCormick had captured the reaper market and so had won the war.

One day in 1860, while Hussey was riding a train in Massachusetts, a little girl asked him to get her a drink of water when the train stopped at a station. Hussey left the train to get the water. As he was reboarding, the train lurched into motion and he lost his footing. Falling beneath the wheels, he was killed instantly. Thus death came to Obed Hussey in his native Massachusetts.

7
Tamer of the Mississippi

ONE EVENING IN THE SPRING OF 1833 when a Mississippi steamboat made fast to a St. Louis wharf, Thomas and Ann Eads, with their thirteen-year-old son James, looked expectantly at the city which would be their new home. After dark they went to their cabin for their last night afloat, intent on disembarking early in the morning. During the night a savage fire broke out and swept the wooden vessel. Passengers and crew fled to safety ashore, lucky to escape with their lives. Everything the Eads family possessed had been aboard the steamboat; now all of it was gone. Young James even lost his shoes in their hasty flight. Barefoot, shivering in the early morning chill, the forlorn youngster could not know that this was only the first in what would be a life-long series of dramatic encounters between him and the river, encounters that would help shape the nation.

James Buchanan Eads had been born in Lawrenceburg, Indiana, on May 23, 1820. His father was a merchant, but not a very successful one. Hoping for better luck in a new location, Thomas Eads moved his family first to Ohio, then to Kentucky, before going on to St. Louis. The Eads' loss of everything they possessed on the very day of arrival was an ill omen.

Because the family was so desperately in need, James gave up school and began hawking apples on the streets of St. Louis. His earnings were slight, but they helped his family. After a few months he found employment as a clerk in the Williams & During Drygoods Company.

Alert, willing, unfailingly polite and well-mannered, James pleased his employers, especially after they saw he was a rapid learner with a logical turn of mind. One of the owners, a man of considerable education, had a fine library and invited James to use it. The boy needed no second invitation. He spent all of his free time immersed in the books, reveling in the knowledge he gained.

In five years young Eads read every book in his employer's library—some of them two and three times. His days were devoted to clerical duties, his evenings to study. It was not the sort of routine that built a strong body. He grew up frail, thin, often plagued with headaches. When one of the firm's customers offered him a job as purser on a riverboat, his employers, though not wanting to lose him, urged him to seize the chance to spend more time out-of-doors for the sake of his health.

Sunshine and fresh air worked wonders for Eads's health. He was fascinated by life on the Mississippi. From captain's bridge to engine room, he applied himself to learning how everything worked—not only the technical aspects of the machinery and equipment, but also the laws of physics on which they were based. The steamboat pilots began to give him an understanding of the mighty river and its complex nature while two years passed.

Landsmen looked at the river and saw it as a trade route down the spine of the nation, or as a threat of massive flooding, or simply as an awesome work of nature. Eads saw all that and much more. He saw the river, together with its tributaries, as the vast drainage basin for the region reaching from the Alleghenies in the east to the Rockies in the west. He studied the river system in all of its seasons and in all of its moods—calm and peaceful, a raging torrent, ice-choked, sometimes abandoning one channel to carve out a fresh one for itself. He came to appreciate the tremendous force created when melting snows and spring rains swirled down into the tributaries, gathered momentum and rushed out into the main river to surge down through the country.

Like the rivermen who taught him to understand

the Mississippi, Eads learned that the waterway extracts a price from those who let their guard down. From the headwaters in the north to the Gulf in the south, the riverbed was littered with the wreckage of vessels. With her tricky currents, her lurking obstructions, her capriciousness, the Mississippi took an enormous and continuous toll.

As he steamed from port to port, Eads speculated about those wrecks. He was tantalized by the thought that each wreck was a potential treasure trove of cargo of all kinds and of still usable engines and equipment. There was a bonanza waiting beneath the surface for one who could obtain it. So Eads began to search for a way of forcing the river to surrender its hidden riches. Slowly he developed a system of salvage, devising techniques and envisioning the kinds of equipment needed.

There were two main elements to his plan. One was a watertight, bell-shaped structure open on the bottom and large enough to contain two men with space sufficient to permit their free movement within the bell. The second was a specially equipped salvage boat. As Eads planned the operation, the boat, with the bell on its deck, would proceed to the wreck site. After anchoring in position over the wreck, the two underwater men would climb into the bell and seat themselves on ledges fastened to its inner wall. After hoses connected to air pumps aboard the boat had been fitted to the bell, it would be winched over the side and lowered onto the wreck. Air pumped down from the salvage boat would keep pressure within the bell high enough to prevent water from flooding in through its open bottom. Working within the protection of the bell, the men would clear sand and silt away from the goods at their feet, attaching lines to whatever was worth salvaging. Once the lines were secure, the bell would be winched back to deck and the lines would be hauled in with their prizes attached.

Eads devoted every spare moment to refining each step in his plans, determining precise specifications and making complete engineering sketches for equipment. In 1842 he was ready for a trial. Obtaining a U.S. patent for the diving bell, he quit his job as purser and consulted the St. Louis boat-building firm of Case & Nelson. Engineers there were impressed with the thoroughness and ingenuity of his plan and optimistic about its success. As a result, Eads and Case & Nelson formed a partnership. Work was immediately begun on the diving bell and on the salvage boat that would support it.

Long before construction was completed, Eads learned of the sinking of a barge in the rapids near Keokuk, Iowa, 200 miles upstream from St. Louis. Aboard the wreck, which lay at a depth of about fifteen feet, was a valuable cargo of lead ingots. The owners, unwilling to abandon the ingots, offered to pay handsomely for recovery of them. The temptation was too great for Eads to resist. He hurried north and surveyed the situation.

What he found was discouraging. The current,

twisting and racing from its descent through the rapids, was dangerously swift. It would have been impossible for a diver, in the crude diving suits then in use, to enter those roiling waters. But the diving bell might be able to cope with the situation. The trouble was it had not yet been completed. Eads decided to try to rig up a substitute bell on the spot.

After hiring a boat, he bought a huge whiskey hogshead and sailed to the site of the wreck. While the crew watched, Eads knocked out the bottom of the hogshead and bored a hole in the top just large enough to admit a hose which would draw down air from a hand pump on deck. Next, he encircled the entire base of the hogshead with weights he hoped were heavy enough to hold it steady on the wreck. Then he attached a sling within the whiskey barrel and climbed inside. The crew tried to talk him out of such folly, insisting that he'd drown. But Eads could not be dissuaded, so they reluctantly winched the hogshead over the side and lowered it into the water.

Perched on his sling, Eads could feel the current surge against the whiskey barrel, straining and trying to wrench it loose and send it tumbling downstream. But the lines linking it to the boat anchored overhead held, and the heavy weights encircling it carried it onto the sunken barge. Despite the close quarters in his jerry-built diving bell, Eads managed to load the ingots into the net he had brought with him. His risky gamble was paying off. The crew could only shake their heads in wonder as, diving repeatedly day after day for the next two weeks, the twenty-two-year-old inventor succeeded in recovering the entire cargo.

Having proved under such adverse circumstances that the concept of the recovery system was sound, there was no doubt that the diving bell and the salvage boat would operate effectively. As soon as work on them was completed, the partnership was able to secure contracts from insurance companies and shipowners for salvage of river wreckage to which they held title. One successful operation followed another.

Alert for ways to improve the operation, Eads continued to build refinements into the system and to invent supporting equipment that would expand its capabilities. A larger, more sophisticated bell and boat followed his first models. With them he even managed to raise entire vessels if they had not been too severely damaged. By the time he was twenty-five he was able to declare that he and his bell had stood on every stretch of the riverbed from above St. Louis all the way to New Orleans.

Once the partnership began turning a comfortable profit, Eads bought his parents a farm in Iowa, and began courting Martha Dillon, daughter of a St. Louis business executive. However, her father stubbornly refused to allow her to marry Eads unless he stopped flitting about the Mississippi and planted his feet firmly on shore in a "respectable" activity. Reluctantly, Eads agreed to leave the river and sold out his interest to his two partners. With the money he decided to establish in St. Louis the nation's first glass factory west of Ohio.

The fact that he knew nothing at all about manufacturing glass did not disturb Eads. He was confident he could learn. He went to Pittsburgh, the country's glass-making center, spending several weeks in concentrated study of the operation of its glass plants, and consulting with experts in all aspects of the processes involved. Ordering necessary equipment and materials and hiring a few key workers to come with him, he returned to St. Louis to build his plant.

As soon as the building was under way, Eads and Martha were married. The marriage was a happy union from the beginning, but the factory was a disaster. Anything that could go wrong at the plant did. Equipment broke down. Accidents occurred. Foremen quit when they were most needed. After two frustrating years of continuing reverses, Eads had no choice but to close the factory, ending up more than $25,000 in debt. In a remarkable display of confidence and affection, his creditors not only agreed to grant him as much time as needed to pay off the debt, but also loaned him additional funds to permit him to repurchase an interest in the ship-salvage enterprise he had founded.

Eads was happy to be back on the Mississippi, back in his element. He devoted himself completely to the river, working harder than ever but enjoying every moment of it because the river was his passion. Wherever there were the worst wrecks, the most challenging salvage problems, he and his diving bell were certain to show up. In a single night in 1849, twenty-nine boats sank in a catastrophic fire that raged along the St. Louis levee. The next morning, while debris still smoldered, Eads began work on the wrecks, remembering the morning so long ago when he was a barefooted, frightened thirteen-year-old experiencing his first riverboat fire. Before he was finished he succeeded in salvaging virtually everything of value from the twenty-nine sunken vessels.

Continually introducing refinements into his equipment, Eads produced a series of improved diving bells and salvage boats. Eventually he was operating four different bells simultaneously, racing from one to the other up and down the Mississippi and its tributaries to see that they and their crews were functioning at top efficiency. He had long since paid off all of his creditors and had built the partnership into a thriving half-million-dollar concern.

As the years passed, he never ceased studying the river and by this time had achieved an unparalleled understanding of it. For him, the giant waterway had become a living thing, with moods, strengths, urges, and quirks he comprehended. His thoughts never strayed far from matters that were in some way related to the river. His wife had long ago accepted the fact that she would always have to share him with the Mississippi. Her only wish was that her husband would not drive himself so hard, because she could see how the long hours and the unremitting work were undermining his health. By 1857 he had to admit that his deteriorating health had turned him into a weak, weary man no longer able to cope with the demands of his job. With infinite regret, he retired from the river for the second time and allowed his wife to fuss over him as she tried to nurse him back to robust health. But even during this period of convalescence he did not abandon the river entirely; he used the time to search out and study scientific and technical data related to all facets of waterways—everything from hydrodynamics and fluviology to marine engineering.

It was President Lincoln who summoned Eads out of retirement. In April, 1861, when Fort Sumter, South Carolina, fell to Confederate forces to herald the outbreak of the Civil War, Lincoln called his military advisers into urgent session to devise the Union's overall strategy. As the talks continued, Lincoln expressed the conviction that the Mississippi was, in his words, "the key to the whole situation," because under Union control it could halt Confederate movement of troops and supplies north and south along the river as well as east and west across it. But the Confederates held a number of strongly fortified points along the waterway and its branches. They would have to be dislodged from their river strongpoints if the Union were to gain the control it sought. When the President's advisers told him Eads understood the

Mississippi better than any other person in America, Lincoln sent for him.

Analyzing the Union's objective in the light of his encyclopedic knowledge of the river's geography and the depth and navigability of its channels, Eads recommended that the federal government build a fleet of shallow-draft, ironclad, steam-propelled gunboats. The proposal was accepted. On August 7, 1861, Union authorities contracted with Eads to construct seven such gunboats for delivery on October 10, only sixty-four days later. The officials knew they were asking the impossible, but they hoped that Eads might, with great luck, not miss the target date by more than a few weeks.

It was foolish to imagine that the task could be completed in anything reasonably close to the allotted time. Designs had to be drawn, engineering specifications calculated. Timber had to be cut and shaped for the hulls. Armor plating had to be rolled and formed. Engines, boilers, auxiliary machinery and equipment had to be fabricated. The deck guns had to be cast and assembled. Only after all these requirements had been satisfied could the construction proper begin.

However, Eads, moving swiftly and decisively, slashed through the chaos and dislocations of war, organizing his enormously complicated undertaking and marshaling resources to meet his needs. In less than two weeks he had forged a network of 4,000 men working on the various components of the ironclads at sites scattered through eight different states. Slowly at first, then at an accelerating pace, the components commenced flowing into central-assembly points where the shipbuilding took place.

Remarkably, on October 12, 1861—only two days past the impossible deadline—Eads completed and launched the *St. Louis,* the first ironclad ever to be launched in American waters. (The widespread notion that that honor belongs to the *Monitor* and the *Merrimac*—either one or the other or the two collectively—is erroneous.) The six additional armored gunboats followed the *St. Louis* into the water in rapid succession.

Never relaxing, Eads immediately designed and built an eighth gunboat, larger, faster, and more powerful than its predecessors. During 1862 and 1863 he constructed six heavily armored attack vessels which included, for the first time anywhere, steam-powered gun turrets of his invention. By using steam to manipulate the weapons, each of the eleven-inch and fifteen-inch guns could be loaded and fired in only forty-five seconds. Eads also designed and launched armored troop transports and heavy mortar boats. His formidable fleet did everything that had been hoped for it—exerting pressure on the Confederacy and denying it ready access to the river to shuttle troops and supplies around, eliminating pockets of Southern resistance, enabling Admiral Farragut to capture Mobile.

The war and the great burdens it had laid on his shoulders left an unmistakable imprint on Eads.

His health, though neither his spirit nor sense of humor, had once again deteriorated. He had lost most of his hair and, sensitive about his baldness, had taken to wearing a small, black skullcap; it was the only sign of vanity ever seen in this modest man.

If his wife thought that with the war ended she could maneuver her husband into a quieter life, she was wrong. Within months after the last shots were fired, Congress passed a bill authorizing the bridging of the Mississippi at St. Louis. It was to be a mammoth project introducing engineering requirements of a scope and magnitude never previously encountered by bridge builders anywhere. A commission of twenty-seven engineers, assembled from across the country, studied the specifications laid down by Congress and declared that the project was not feasible, that the technology did not exist to build such an unprecedented structure.

Eads analyzed the proposed bridge against his own knowledge of construction and against his unique understanding of the riverbed and of the stresses the current would exert against the bridge abutments. He declared that he disagreed with the commission's opinion. It was his belief that the techniques could be devised to meet Congress's requirements satisfactorily. The company that had been awarded the construction contract designated Eads the engineer-in-charge.

The challenges were awesome. The bridge was to consist of three giant arches, the central arch to stretch 520 feet between its supporting piers, the side arches to span only slightly smaller distances from each bank to the river piers supporting the central arch. The two river piers themselves were to be huge granite towers, larger than any previously built.

Eads commenced with the piers. To make their construction possible, he created special watertight caissons within which crews using mining techniques could sink shafts through 90 feet of sand and gravel to secure firm footing on solid bedrock. Once bedrock was reached, they could commence erection of the two giant granite structures.

As soon as the pier work was proceeding smoothly, Eads turned to the intimidating problems posed by the spans. It was not only the length of the arches that taxed his ingenuity, but also their enormous weight. So great was the weight that its pressure would actually cause a slight compression in the steel from which the arches would be fabricated. This meant that the spans had to be made slightly larger than the actual distances they would bridge, so that after compression had taken place they would be the precise size desired. Making long, precise calculations, he concluded that each span would require a design length two and one-half inches greater than its required length in place.

After completing the design phase of the arches, Eads had to devise techniques for the erection of such unprecedentedly long spans. Once again he demonstrated a novel approach. Starting on opposite sides of the river, he began forming his arch out over the water toward the pier nearest it, supporting the projecting construction with thick cables slung from temporary towers on shore. Meanwhile, out in the river he had crews on the two piers commencing to build outward from both sides of each pier, the construction on the shoreward-facing side to meet and mate at the midway point with the span growing toward it from shore; the construction from the two inward-facing sides to meet and mate in mid-river to form the central arch. His method of supporting the spans being built outward from the piers was unusual and effective —he simply linked the construction on the two sides of the pier by temporary cables passed over the top of the pier. In this way each side balanced and supported the other.

The bridge was a brilliant feat of engineering. It was dedicated with fanfare on July 4, 1874. His wife thought that now, with this great work a reality, Eads would finally relax and take care of himself. She was mistaken. Her husband left almost at once for the other end of the Mississippi, where another great undertaking was shaping up.

Sandbars at the mouth of the river had become an acute problem for shipping, preventing deep-draft vessels from entering from the Gulf and imperiling smaller craft attempting to negotiate the tricky passage. The waterway was a vital supply route for the nation's rapidly growing mid-section, and the need to open it to hazard-free navigation was urgent. Congress had directed the U.S. Army Corps of Engineers to formulate plans to clear the river mouth for shipping. The Corps had come up with the recommendation that the sandbar problem be sidestepped by digging a canal to bypass the mouth, creating a link from the Gulf to the river at an upstream point above the sandbars.

Opposing the Corps's proposal, Eads asserted that the matter could be resolved without abandoning the river to the sandbars and building a costly bypass. He was convinced, he said, that he could create conditions whereby the Mississippi would remove the sandbars all by itself. Skeptics laughed and labeled him a crackpot. But Congress, well aware that Eads was far from being a crackpot, asked him to explain his concept for their consideration.

What Eads proposed was the narrowing of the shipping channel through the mouth of the river by building long jetties down each side to pinch the water into a more confined passageway. If the jetties were spaced the proper distance apart to create sufficient increase in the flow rate, he reasoned that the accelerated current would exert a scouring effect upon the sandbars to scrape them from the riverbed and prevent the formation of new ones in the future. Assured by Eads that his radical proposal was entirely feasible, Congress—though still somewhat dubious—gave him a go-ahead on his plan despite contrary advice from the Corps of Engineers.

Eads commenced work on the South Pass, one of three obstructed channels through the river's mouth. He designed two two-mile-long jetties. The underwater portion of each jetty was an open gridwork of woven willows, ballasted with rock to anchor it to the river bottom. Silt swirling through the grid openings quickly began filling the interior and compacting into a solid mass. Along the firm base which he created in this way, Eads laid a masonry buttress rising high enough above the river to contain it at flood tide. Exactly as he had calculated, the compression of the river speeded the flow to the point that a scouring action was induced along the riverbed.

In 1875, when jetty construction had been initiated, the South Pass was choking on two monster sandbars, one rising to 14 feet below the surface of the river, the other to within 8 feet of the surface. A federal inspection team in 1879 reported to Congress that the Eads jetties had caused the Mississippi to self-scour itself to a depth of 30 feet through the South Pass. This remarkable result was achieved at a cost only one half that of the bypass canal urged by the Corps of Engineers.

Ships which previously had been prevented from entering the Mississippi at once took advantage of the access they were now granted. All along the river, commerce flourished. Before the jetties, New Orleans had ranked eleventh among U.S. cities in the size of the exports leaving its docks. After the jetties, New Orleans shot up to second place among exporting cities in the United States.

Eating crow, if not with relish at least with a commendable show of good grace, the Corps of Engineers conceded that James B. Eads had opened a whole new chapter in river and harbor operations. The Corps offered no word of dissent when directed by Congress to introduce the Eads concept to other threatened sections of the river system.

Eads was now exhausted. The black skullcap which had become his trademark served to emphasize the pallor of his drawn, lined face. He wanted, and he needed, a long period of rest away from strain and pressure. But this was denied him. From every quarter came urgent requests for his counsel on waterway problems; he could not bring himself to refuse.

At the urging of Jacksonville's municipal authorities, he went to Florida to study the St. John's River and lay out a program to improve its mouth. Then, in response to a plea from the governor of California, he devised a method of dealing with problems of the Sacramento River. In 1881 he went north to advise the Canadian government on ways to enhance Toronto Harbor, and the next year he went south to counsel the Mexicans on how to deal with the harbors at Veracruz and Tampico. He sailed for Europe when the British sought his guidance on construction of a canal at Manchester, the Germans his advice on improving their Baltic ports, the Austro-Hungarians his views on matters related to the Danube and Theiss Rivers. Then he returned to the United States, where Texas officials were

116

anxious for him to design the reconstruction of the entrance to Galveston Harbor. Next, the Emperor of Brazil summoned him to South America for consultations concerning harbors in his country.

The strains of these unremitting demands from around the world were too much for Eads. His health became a matter of grave concern. In January 1887, at the insistence of his doctors, he sailed to Nassau in the Bahamas to recuperate.

Sitting in the Bahamian sun, Eads had time to reflect on the surprising twists and turns of his incredible career. From the time he had commenced as a thirteen-year-old hawker of apples in St. Louis, life had been exciting, demanding, challenging, and he was grateful for every moment of it. His passion for the Mississippi had led him eventually to council chambers around the world, had brought him honors he could never have imagined: an honorary degree from the University of Missouri, though he had never gone beyond elementary school; membership in the National Academy of Sciences; expressions of gratitude from President Lincoln, Congress, foreign dignitaries. If he had given deeply of himself to the Mississippi—walked its bottom, bridged its surface, invented its warships, altered its flow—the Mississippi in its turn had given deeply of itself to him and he was content.

In March, three months after he arrived in Nassau, sixty-seven-year-old James Buchanan Eads—the man who conquered rivers as no man before him or since—died sitting under the Bahamian sun with his black skullcap perched on his head.

8
The Woman
Who Saved Children

IN POUGHKEEPSIE, NEW YORK, SPRING
flowers were in full bloom on a sunny day in 1880.
In an upstairs bedroom of a house on a quiet,
tree-lined street, Mrs. Orlando Baker was getting
her six-year-old daughter, Sara Josephine, ready
for a garden party to which both mother and
daughter had been invited. When the girl was
dressed to her satisfaction, Mrs. Baker sent her
downstairs to wait while she put on her own party
clothes.

Josephine (she was an adult before she started
calling herself Sara Josephine) wandered out to the
sidewalk to wait in the sunshine. The hushed street
was deserted. Then Josephine heard footsteps. She

looked up and saw that a little black girl was approaching. When the other girl drew abreast, she halted. Wordlessly, the two children stared at one another, each acutely aware of the contrast in their appearances. The white child, primped for party-going, was all starchy crispness and lacy flounces and bright ribbons. The black child—thin, barefoot, wearing a shapeless dress that was torn and faded—stared at the other's clothes with an expression in which longing was clearly evident.

Moments passed as the two children studied one another, not with animosity but with the frank curiosity of the young. Then, there on the sunny sidewalk, Josephine commenced to undress. As the other girl's eyes opened wide in amazement, she removed everything she wore—dress, petticoat, underwear, shoes, stockings—folding it all into a neat pile. Still wordless, Josephine handed the clothing to the astounded black girl. Uttering a cry that could have been a sob or a laugh or a little of each, the girl whirled and fled down the street tightly clutching her gift. Josephine, naked, turned and re-entered the house. Somehow, her mother—when she overcame her initial shock— was able to understand her daughter's impulsive act.

The incident was a foretaste of the future, for Sara Josephine Baker was to become a champion of the disadvantaged and was to make major contributions to their welfare. This would be especially true of her contributions to children. She would, before

120

she was through, introduce changes that would alter the lives of children everywhere.

But all of that lay in the future. During her years in Poughkeepsie, the only hint of things to come was the incident with the little black girl. Otherwise Josephine was an active, happy, outgoing child, full of energy and mischief. If she was in any way different from other neighborhood girls, it was that she was far less interested than they in playing with dolls and jumping rope and more interested in tomboy activities. She was especially good at baseball, so the boys, stifling their male chauvinism only because she could more than hold her own with them, included her in their games. But she was fondest of fishing, a sport she shared with her lawyer-father. Even after she entered Miss Thomas' school, a staid, strict institution, she managed to slip away frequently to fish along the banks of the Hudson.

The carefree days came to an abrupt end in 1890 when her father was fatally stricken with typhoid fever. After his estate was settled, few financial resources remained to sustain his family. Almost overnight, Josephine's lighthearted youth had fled. It was time now to contemplate the situation through adult eyes and to come up with adult solutions. While Josephine mourned her father, she, with her mother, considered how best to prepare herself for a gainful occupation. Gain alone held little interest for her. She discovered something about herself she had never before consciously realized: she was a giver, not a taker. She had a need to give, an urge to serve society in some practical, productive way. Always her thoughts returned to one career: the practice of medicine.

Everyone tried to dissuade her. Her mother, the family doctor, relatives and friends, all urged her to turn to a field that was more attainable. They pointed out that the route to a medical degree was long and difficult. More to the point, they emphasized that medicine was by tradition a "man's profession," that prejudice against women doctors was so widespread that the few who succeeded in entering the field faced a professional life burdened with rebuffs and frustrations. But all found, as others would later discover, that when Sara Josephine Baker was determined to do something, she could not be stopped.

The first barrier to be surmounted was a college education as a preliminary to medical school. The Baker financial resources simply could not be stretched to cover both college and medical school. Undaunted, Josephine proposed to give herself her own college education and then take the formidable New York State regents' examinations. Passing them would give her academic credentials enabling her to skip college and apply directly for admission to medical school.

Borrowing books from libraries and family friends, Josephine shut out the rest of the world. For more than a year books were her only constant companions. Then she sat for the regents' examinations, which proved as rigorous as reputed. Even though she felt she had acquitted herself reasonably well, she awaited the results nervously. At last she joyfully received word that she had passed, that her self-study had been accepted as the equivalent of four years on a college campus. Then she applied to and was accepted by the Women's Medical School of the New York Infirmary for Women and Children.

Medical school was arduous, but Josephine had not expected it to be otherwise. She applied herself with the same degree of intensity that she had devoted to her preparation for the regents' examinations. She did not merely keep up with her college-trained classmates, she led them. When she received her medical degree in 1898, she ranked second among the eighteen new doctors who graduated with her.

Her immediate concern was to find a hospital that would accept her for the necessary year of practical experience as an intern. Hospital doors opened reluctantly for women interns, no matter how well they had fared in medical school. The only opening she was able to secure was an internship in Boston's New England Hospital for Women and Children.

An intern's life is, at best, a time of trial and tribulation. Occupying the bottom rung of the medical ladder, the intern works the longest hours and the meanest schedules of all the hospital's doctors, is assigned to the drudgery chores and the most irksome cases, and is constantly at the beck and call of the resident physicians. But it is also a time to learn the practical side of medicine under the guidance of experienced doctors. So Dr. Baker endured the tribulations willingly and uncomplainingly, grateful for the opportunity to perfect her professional techniques. She even managed to find the time and energy to work in a public clinic in the Boston slums. In many ways her slum work was the more satisfying of her two jobs, because the patients she cared for there were not only sick, they were also desperately poor and disadvantaged.

In 1900, her days as an intern ended, Dr. Baker moved to New York, where she set up a private office and waited for patients to knock on her door. It was a long, lonely wait, punctuated by only an occasional knock. She was experiencing the widespread prejudice against women doctors, learning firsthand how deeply rooted was the absurd belief that they lacked the competence of males to deal with the sick. At the end of her first full year of private practice, she had earned the pitifully meager total of $185. But what disturbed her most was that she was being denied the chance to fully utilize the medical skills she had acquired. How ridiculous, she thought, that the city is full of sick people who obtain little or no professional care, while I am ready and anxious to provide that care but cannot reach them.

Seeking a means of bridging the gulf between herself and the ill whom she could serve, she sought and obtained a post with the New York City health department as a medical inspector. Two factors enabled her to get the job. The first was that it paid only $30 a month, so there was no competition for the post. The second was that she subtly de-emphasized the fact she was a woman, cutting her hair short in a mannish bob and wearing plain tailored suits with blouses and neckties. It amused her to compare her severely businesslike on-the-job costume with the flounces and lace her mother had dressed her in as a child.

Despite Dr. Baker's efforts to appear business-like and her insistence that she neither wished nor would accept special consideration because of her sex, many of her male colleagues did not bother to hide their bias. Usually it took the form of comments that were intended to belittle and annoy; these she simply ignored. Sometimes it manifested itself in unpleasant assignments, and these she accepted without giving her male col-leagues the satisfaction of hearing her protest the unfairness of the situation.

The most serious harassment came in the sum-mer of 1902 when Dr. Baker was assigned to survey health conditions in "Hell's Kitchen," a rough, tough, rundown section of West Side Manhattan that even hardened male inspectors tried to avoid. She took on the assignment calmly, because she neither feared slums nor was a stranger to them, having worked in the slums of Boston, and because she knew that it was there that the need for medical assistance was the greatest.

For the next six months New York's sole woman

medical inspector spent every day in "Hell's Kitchen"—humoring drunks, turning aside street bullies, reassuring those who suspected her intentions—as she resolutely combed through one decaying, overcrowded tenement after another, seeking the ill and the infirm and seeing to it that they received the care they needed but had not been getting. She was especially successful in discovering sick infants whose illnesses had been dismissed by their parents as "just the wailing that all babies do." In several instances she found children with contagious diseases. Her prompt diagnosis and removal of the child for treatment in hospital facilities prevented the disease from sweeping through the vulnerable tenement families.

Her performance in "Hell's Kitchen" eroded the bias she had been encountering among co-workers. None of them could fault her handling of the long, tough assignment, and several must have admitted—although only within the privacy of their own minds—that they would have been hard-pressed to have done as well.

More and more with the passage of time, Dr. Baker was drawn to the plight of young children, for they were the most defenseless, exposed, and afflicted segment of the city's population. The appalling infant mortality statistics of the early 1900s told the story in stark and frightening terms. In the summer months, the height of the "sick season" for youngsters, as many as 1,500 babies died in New York City each week. This shocking death toll was not peculiar to New York alone; the infant mortality rate was depressingly high throughout the country—in fact, throughout the world—especially in the large, crowded cities. Josephine Baker resolved to find a way to alleviate the situation. First, though, there was an emergency to be dealt with: an outbreak of typhoid fever.

For years the city had been struggling to contain the recurring outbreaks of typhoid, a painful disease that was often fatal. Once it was realized that effective counter-measures had to commence with attacking the disease at its source, medical inspectors had made major efforts to dry up the prime breeding places for the infection: contaminated water and contaminated milk. Slowly, they had made headway in the undertaking to chop off typhoid at its roots—the numbers of typhoid victims leveled off and began to diminish. Then, in 1907, the disease once again broke through the city's defenses and ran rampant through New York. The health department declared an emergency and created a special task force to combat the outbreak. Dr. Baker, who was just completing her stint in "Hell's Kitchen," was named a member of that task force. It was an assignment that had a deep, special meaning for her, because typhoid had killed her father.

Mobilizing all of its resources, the task force organized the city's doctors, nurses, and hospital facilities into a coordinated undertaking to care for the victims. Striking at the same time at the source of the disease, it dispatched teams throughout the city to search for and eliminate all contaminated water and milk supplies. Even though the teams wiped out these breeding grounds of typhoid, the epidemic continued to ravage the city. Clearly, it was being spread by another means. To Dr. Baker there was only one likely answer: a human carrier, an individual whose body harbored the typhoid micro-organisms but who himself had such high natural immunity that he was unaffected by and unaware of the disease-causing germs he carried. Thus, the carrier would be the unwitting instrument through which the disease was spread.

There also had to be another link in the chain: a way for the micro-organisms to hitch a ride between the carrier in whom they lurked and the victim in whom they could wreak their havoc. In other words, the victim's food or drink had to become exposed to the carrier so that the germs could contaminate it before it was consumed. If Dr. Baker was right, then somewhere among the millions in the city would be an employee of a food processing or distribution center of some kind who was unknowingly spreading typhoid on a massive scale. The other task-force members agreed that this was the probable answer to the disease's obstinate persistence. They immediately launched a massive manhunt for the suspected carrier.

The search was intensive and exhausting. It

required interviewing hundreds of survivors and their families to try to find a common thread, a similarity in their movements and habits that might point the way. Addresses of the victims were plotted on huge maps to determine if they were clustered in specific sections of the city. Doctors examined thousands of employees of food-processing plants, slaughterhouses, dairies, and other food-handling facilities. In the end, the sustained manhunt led—not to a man—but to a woman: Mary Mallon, quickly dubbed "Typhoid Mary" by the press. She was both a carrier and a restaurant cook, a combination that was devastating for thousands who had eaten in establishments where she had worked. With the discovery of Typhoid Mary and her elimination from the food chain, the disease subsided and Dr. Baker's task force disbanded.

Sara Josephine Baker was by this time a well-known figure in New York medical circles, admired for her professional expertise and her boundless energy, respected for her no-nonsense approach to public health. How well she was regarded was demonstrated in 1907, the same year as the typhoid outbreak, when she was appointed New York's assistant health commissioner. The elevation of a woman to such an important post was unprecedented, and it indicated how thoroughly she had stilled the voices that had been raised against her initially on the basis of her sex.

Now, as assistant commissioner, Dr. Baker had

greater scope to move aggressively and innovatively against the shockingly high rate of infant mortality. In the spring of 1908 she formulated a program calculated to come to grips with the alarming situation, and she won City Hall's approval for a trial of her concept.

Assembling a team of thirty nurses, she schooled them in her test program. Once she had them trained to her satisfaction, she led them into a poor, overcrowded section of lower Manhattan to put her plan into operation. Knocking on doors in the squalid tenements, she and her nurses pioneered what would later become known as preventive medicine and public health education. They taught mothers how to care for their children properly, healthfully. They explained the hows and the whys of sanitation, nutrition, ventilation; showed how to recognize the early-warning signs of all of the common childhood diseases. Although milk was starting to become widely available in bottles rather than only in open containers, it was still unpasteurized, so they encouraged mothers to breast-feed their infants. Patiently the nurses made suggestions and answered questions as they tried to substitute fact for ignorance and superstition.

At the end of the summer the Baker project was evaluated for its effectiveness, and the results were startling. Infant deaths in the section where Dr. Baker and her nurses had operated were reduced by a whopping 1,200 below the number of fatalities for the identical period in the preceding year. In every other section of the city, infant deaths remained at the same high level as in the previous year. The test had proved an unqualified success.

Confronting the municipal leaders with the solid proof that her ideas were eminently sound, Dr. Baker now argued persuasively for the establishment of her child-health program on a permanent, city-wide basis. Outspoken in her presentation, she cited facts and figures that drove home the enormity of the misery that was the lot of so many of the city's children. Her "their-blood-is-on-your-hands" bluntness made the officials squirm; she won their approval. The city established the Bureau of Child Hygiene, with Dr. Baker as its director. This was the first public agency anywhere in the world created solely as a guardian of the health of children. In the years that followed, every state in the Union, as well as the federal government and many foreign governments, would follow Dr. Baker's lead and establish agencies modeled after hers.

Being the first means that there are no precedents to follow as a guideline. This pleased Dr. Baker, because she wanted to exercise her own originality and this gave her the latitude she needed to do so. One after the other, she conceived and instituted imaginative, progressive measures that would later become the blueprint for future child-health agencies. She sent nurses into homes throughout the city to show families proper health procedures, initiated a system of regular health examinations for students in city schools, distributed health-care pamphlets written in clear, easy-to-understand language. Because so many women gave birth at home, with only a midwife in attendance, Dr. Baker initiated a free training program to raise the level of performance of midwives and, for the first time, she required that they prove their competence and obtain licenses in order to practice.

At strategic locations throughout the city Dr. Baker established clinics where mothers could secure routine medical attention for their children and could obtain wholesome, pure milk for them. Turning to the administrative procedures governing admission to hospitals, she streamlined them and eliminated much of the red tape so that they would not be so intimidating to immigrant families or to the poorly educated.

Little escaped Sara Josephine Baker's alert eye. Noting that many infants were being blinded in accidents that occurred during the application of eye-drops at time of birth, she invented an accident-proof dispenser for the medication. Likewise, when she found that much of the clothing then in use for babies was unhealthful—binding and chafing or preventing proper ventilation, and in some cases even causing death by strangulation—she designed new clothing that was both comfortable and safe. Her designs were so superior that they were quickly adopted by commercial manufacturers.

All of these innovations had a marked effect on

the health of the city's children. Year by year the mortality rate grew less appalling. As word of this new, highly successful approach to child care spread, speaking requests showered in on Dr. Baker from all parts of the country and abroad. Although already committed to a heavy work schedule, she accepted as many speaking engagements as possible, spurred on by the knowledge that she was helping to improve child health far beyond the borders of New York.

In 1916 the Medical School of New York University asked Dr. Baker to deliver a series of lectures on child care to students and faculty of the institution. She agreed—a commitment that eventually became annual lectures for the next fifteen years—but she imposed one condition. Her condition was that the university accept her as a student in its new graduate course in public health, a course to which no woman had yet been admitted. The university agreed, and in 1917 she became the first woman to earn a doctorate in public health. Thus, although she had never attended college as an undergraduate, she had the unique distinction of having earned two doctorates.

Asked by the federal government in 1922 to be the U.S. representative to the Health Committee of the League of Nations, she obtained a leave of absence from her post as director of the Bureau of Child Hygiene. As in every other undertaking she had ever attempted, she brought to her new responsibilities dedication, intelligence, and imagination. She also took with her to the Health Committee's sessions in Geneva something else that turned out to be quite useful—the plain-spoken, realistic point of view that she had honed razor-sharp in her years of dealing with New York City politicians; it helped to counter-balance some of the high-flown, irrelevant rhetoric of many of her League of Nations colleagues.

After several months it became evident that the work of the Health Committee would not be concluded as speedily as she had hoped, so she reluctantly retired from the directorship of the Bureau of Child Hygiene in order to be free to continue in her League role. Of all the praise she received as she turned the Bureau over to her successor, the tribute that pleased her most was an expression of gratitude for having reduced New York's baby deaths by a startling 50 percent, giving it a lower infant mortality rate than any other major city in the world.

In 1924, her work with the League finally concluded, Dr. Baker returned from Geneva. But she had been too active for too long to simply fade into quiet retirement. She served as health adviser to a number of public agencies on state and federal levels and wrote scores of child-care articles for professional journals. In 1935–36 she served as president of the American Medical Women's Association.

Having devoted all of her adult years to an unremitting battle for the lives of others, Sara

Josephine Baker lost the fight for her own life in 1945, succumbing to cancer at the age of seventy-two.

9
The Color of Blood

CHARLES R. DREW WAS VERY LIGHT-skinned. His hair had a reddish tinge. He could have passed for white. In fact, several of his white friends at Amherst College, seeking to shield him from the prejudices and indignities to which blacks were so frequently subjected, urged him to take the easy way out and list himself in the records as Caucasian. "Who would know?" they asked.

"I would know," Drew always replied. "For me that would not be the easy way out, because it would make me sacrifice my integrity and pride to the stupidity of the bigots. That would bring me down to their level and I won't do that."

Washington, D.C., where Drew was born in

1904, was still a rigidly segregated city, despite the fact it was the nation's capital. His parents—his father, a carpet layer, and his mother, a schoolteacher—had refused to let injustice defeat them, and they were determined that injustice would not defeat their children. They created in Charlie—the nickname that would stay with him all his life—a sense of values and of self-worth, a belief that the blindness of society must not also become his blindness. They taught him to approach life with confidence, hope, and the resolve to use his talents to the full to achieve the best of which he was capable.

How well he absorbed these lessons became abundantly apparent in high school. He always gave his best, whether in the classroom or on the athletic field. And his best was very impressive. Academically, he ranked up among the school's leaders. Athletically, he was *the* leader. Football, baseball, basketball, track—he starred in all. In 1922 Amherst College offered him a scholarship on the basis of both his athletic and academic accomplishments.

The distance from Washington, D.C., to Amherst, Massachusetts, is only some 400 miles. But in 1922 the distance from segregated Dunbar High to Amherst College was much more than merely a matter of miles. For the first time in his life Charlie Drew was a member of an affluent, white student body, selected from among the cream of the applicants for admission to that prestigious institution. Many had graduated from fine private academies especially geared to preparing students to meet the high standards of colleges like Amherst. None of this intimidated him. He simply took everything in stride and continued being himself, doing his best.

Even during his freshman year Charlie Drew began making his mark at Amherst. In classroom, lecture hall, and laboratory, the faculty quickly recognized his bright intellect and logical, retentive mind. What pleased his professors most was that he sought knowledge for the satisfaction of knowing rather than out of the need to pass courses. He was the kind of perceptive, diligent student who makes professors happy that they undertook to become teachers. Moreover, he was personable, likeable, popular among his classmates.

If Charlie Drew pleased Amherst's professors, he also pleased its coaches. His performance on the playing fields was extraordinary. An all-around athlete—fast, well-coordinated, skillful, powerful—he played with the important attributes of fluid grace and intelligence. In his junior year he was named an All-Eastern football halfback. In his senior year he captained the track team.

When he graduated in 1926, it was clear that he and Amherst had been good for each other. At the graduation ceremonies the student body and faculty applauded enthusiastically when he was presented his bachelor of arts degree. And they cheered as he was called to the podium to receive the coveted Mossman Trophy for the outstanding contributions he had made to the college during his four years there.

A comfortable, secure future was within easy grasp if he wished to reach out for it. With his academic credentials and outstanding athletic career, he could easily become a high school or even a college coach. But Charlie Drew had never seriously considered that option. He wanted to become a doctor. He knew how long and rough the road would be, especially for a black man, but he had never shunned challenge nor sold himself short.

Then, as now, a medical education was costly. Drew set out to earn enough to pay his initial tuition fees, accepting a post teaching biology and chemistry at Morgan State College in Baltimore. He also served on the coaching staff. In two years he had accumulated enough of a nest egg to get him started in medical school. He applied for admission to McGill University, a highly respected institution in Montreal, and was accepted in its medical program.

The McGill curriculum was rigorous, leaving little time for sports, but Drew was too much the athlete to give up participation completely. Limiting himself to track, he became a member of the McGill team, where he turned in sparkling performances, ultimately being named team captain and winning Canadian championships in the high and low hurdles, the high jump, and the broad jump.

Out of necessity, he also served from time to time as a free-lance referee at local sports meets to earn something to slow the alarming rate at which his nest egg was melting away. Then an American foundation granted him a scholarship sufficient to pay his tuition, and his money worries were eased.

It was during his second year at McGill that Drew met Dr. John Beattie, a medical instructor. It was a meeting that was to prove overwhelmingly significant for each. The two liked each other from the start, respected each other's quick mind and quiet sense of humor. Dr. Beattie was only a few years older than Charlie Drew, so they were able to talk as contemporaries and they took delight in their long bull sessions—discussions that ranged over whatever claimed their interests at the moment, but that usually involved some aspect of medical science.

At some point in his discussions with Beattie, Drew decided to follow the lead of his friend and point himself toward a career as a medical researcher and teacher, as Beattie had done, rather than as a physician in private practice. Private practice was the accepted route toward financial reward and material comforts, Drew knew. But research and teaching—searching for new knowledge and helping to spread those fresh insights among those who could utilize them for the benefit of society—were goals he prized more.

Because Beattie was involved in research in blood chemistry, it was probably inevitable that Drew would also focus his attention on it. For both of them the fascination of blood lay in the fact that there were still tantalizing gaps in medical science's understanding of this vital fluid. True, giant strides had been made since the days when physicians routinely applied leeches to patients to drain "bad" blood from them, seldom benefiting the patient and often simply bleeding him to death. Yet many puzzling questions still remained to be answered. Finding the answers to those questions about the nature of blood would create a basis for raising the quality of health care.

The days were barely long enough for all that Charlie Drew crammed into them. The medical-school academic load is by itself a tough enough challenge, but in addition to the lectures, the lab work, and the mountains of textbooks to be mastered, in addition to captaining the track team and performing brilliantly with it, he somehow managed to study all the technical data on blood chemistry that he could find in the medical library. It was a demanding, eighteen-hour-a-day schedule, but he thrived on it, earning membership in the university's scholastic honor society to accompany his victories on the track.

In the late spring of 1933, Drew and 137 other medical students at McGill reached the climax of their five years of study: the gruelling series of examinations that constituted the final, critical assessment of their worthiness to be granted medical degrees. When the results were posted, Charlie

Drew learned that he had scored second highest of all who had sat for the examinations. He was granted not one, but two coveted degrees: doctor of medicine and master of surgery.

Dr. Drew—how thrilled he was the first time he was addressed by his new, hard-won title—did not hesitate when Montreal General Hospital offered him his year of internship at that institution. What made Montreal General so attractive to him was not only that it was a fine hospital, but also that it had installed a modern blood-chemistry laboratory and that his old friend, John Beattie, was using it for a research project he was conducting.

The relationship between them that had commenced as teacher and student had altered over the years to become one of professional equals, because by now, thanks to his intensive study of the subject, Drew had acquired a sophisticated understanding of the nature of blood.

Blood is an enormously complex substance—part liquid, part solid. The solid portion contains red blood cells, white blood cells, and platelets. The red cells serve as the mechanism by which oxygen, injected into the bloodstream by the lungs, is parceled out to the tissue in the body; they also serve as the mechanism for removing carbon dioxide from tissue. The white cells operate as a defense against certain diseases. Platelets help blood to coagulate at the mouth of a wound to halt bleeding.

The liquid portion of the blood, plasma, is 91

percent water, but the remaining 9 percent of the plasma is a remarkable mix of various proteins, gases, salts, hormones, acids and other substances. The role of many of the materials present in normal blood was not clearly understood in 1933, and even today considerable mystery still surrounds some of them.

What was clearly understood, then as now, is that to sustain life the body must maintain its blood supply at an acceptable level. In most cases, the sudden loss of about a pint of blood out of the adult body's normal six quarts poses no threat because the body manufactures more to compensate for the loss. But sudden losses much in excess of one pint cannot be replaced by the body rapidly enough to prevent putting the victim's life in jeopardy. The solution to this problem is transfusion, restoring blood supply to its normal level by injecting into the veins blood from a source outside the body of the patient.

In 1934, when Drew and Beattie were trying to unravel some of the mysteries of blood, transfusion had come a very long way from 1668 when French police arrested a doctor who had transfused lamb's blood into a patient in an experiment that killed him. But it was not until the mid-1880s that medical science had accepted the view that if transfusion were to be developed into a useful, safe technique, it had to be restricted to human blood. And it was only in the early 1900s that transfusion had become reliable with the discovery that all human blood is not identical, that it is divided into four groups, each of which differs from the others in only one respect: its red cells are slightly different from the red cells in each of the other groups. For purposes of convenience the groups were labeled A, B, AB, and O.

Probing for meaning in the finding that blood is divided into four types, researchers had learned that only a person whose blood type is AB can safely receive blood of any type; but that only A blood must go to those whose blood type is A; only B blood must go to B types; and only O blood to O types. Failure to properly match transfused blood to that of the recipient causes red cells to clump together in his blood vessels, creating an obstruction that can lead to death.

But if doctors now had an understanding of the fundamental requirements for safe transfusion, the transfusion itself was a tense and chaotic process. When an emergency arose requiring immediate transfusion, doctors would hastily draw a blood sample from the patient and rush it to the lab for analysis to determine its type. Meanwhile, an urgent call was issued for volunteers to donate blood; as soon as they responded to the appeal, samples had to be drawn from these prospective donors and rushed to the lab for typing. After blood matches were found between volunteers and patients, the actual transfusions could commence. Often several hours would elapse before this complicated sequence of events could be completed.

The delay frequently had fatal consequences for the patient.

Medical science had so far been unable to devise a satisfactory system of collecting and storing blood in advance of need so that in an emergency it would be instantly available for transfusion. Refrigeration had been tried, but it was useless because it extended the life of the stored blood by only a few hours before it deteriorated and had to be discarded. Freezing had also been attempted, but nobody had yet found a way to keep the freezing from destroying the red cells.

But there must be a way to store blood safely, Charlie Drew kept telling himself, a way to deposit blood in a medical "bank" that would protect and preserve it for instant withdrawal in time of need. Throughout 1934 and 1935, as he completed his internship and then a year as resident physician at Montreal General, he continued his blood research, seeking clues to aid in development of storage techniques.

With his time at Montreal General drawing to a close, Dr. Drew was invited by Howard University, a noted black college in Washington, D.C., to join the faculty of its medical school. He could not turn his back on Howard because he felt a deep-seated obligation to contribute whatever he could toward the training of other black doctors. So, not forsaking his devotion to blood research but merely putting it aside for the time being, he joined the Howard faculty.

In 1938 Dr. Drew was offered a Rockefeller fellowship for research at Columbia-Presbyterian Medical Center in New York City. To be chosen for such an honor was a signal mark of recognition that was flattering, but what made the offer truly irresistible was the fact that the Center's highly respected director of research, Dr. John Scudder, was then conducting a broad-scale investigation of blood. Thus Charlie Drew would once again be able to devote himself actively to the line of scientific inquiry that had gripped him for so long. He promptly accepted.

Drew discussed with Scudder his blood-bank concept, and they agreed that Drew should head up a small team to work on it. Even though refrigeration had so far proven unsatisfactory as a means of storage, Drew felt it merited further examination. He knew that it was the breakdown of red cells under refrigeration that caused the spoilage, but he had also learned that red cells, even unrefrigerated, had a tendency to break down unless they were handled gently. That suggested one possible approach to him—the design of containers that would cushion stored blood to protect it from shock. Another matter he wanted to explore was whether or not red cells reacted in the same way to all degrees of refrigeration or whether a particular temperature could be found at which the cells remained viable longer.

Dr. Drew and his team embarked on a series of experiments he devised to follow these and other lines of investigation. Most of their experiments turned out to be frustrating blind alleys. But occasionally their efforts showed distinct promise. One exciting discovery they made was that adding a small quantity of sodium citrate to blood that was maintained at a constant temperature of 4 degrees Centigrade would extend the useful life of the blood by several days. Ultimately, Drew and his assistants were able to evolve a system of storage, processing, and refrigeration that appeared to preserve blood safely for as long as two weeks.

The next logical step was to test the stored blood on humans. Well aware of the inescapable element of risk, Dr. Drew outlined his plan to Dr. Scudder and proposed establishment of a test blood bank at Presbyterian Hospital. After carefully evaluating all the research data and the methods proposed for operation of the bank, Scudder endorsed the plan and submitted it to the hospital board for approval. Authorization was granted for a four-month trial of a pilot blood bank.

Testing of the Drew blood bank commenced under tight controls. Blood samples were drawn from patients before they were transfused, and again after transfusion was completed. The before-and-after samples were minutely examined and compared for differences, however slight. The patients themselves were monitored closely and continuously for reaction to the transfused blood. The findings demonstrated beyond question that blood stored and handled under the Drew techniques was entirely safe for at least one week. After one week there was an accelerating tendency toward breakdown of red cells. The decision was made to use blood only during its first week of storage and to discard any not used by the end of the seventh day. The blood bank was hailed as a success.

Dr. Drew should have been content because he had accomplished what he had set out to do—he had created a blood-bank system that worked—but he was not satisfied to rest on his laurels. There was more that needed doing. There were still un-answered, vexing questions, still new avenues he wanted to explore.

If, he reasoned, breakdown of red cells makes it prudent to avoid storing blood beyond one week, could one eliminate the problem by removing the troublesome red cells prior to storage, simply retaining the plasma alone? Would transfusion of plasma only, instead of whole blood, work? How would the body respond to plasma transfusion? These provocative questions tantalized him. He had to learn the answers.

Retaining the bank's seven-day-old blood that would otherwise be discarded, Dr. Drew separated the plasma from it. Then he subjected the plasma to every method of analysis and testing that he could devise. After he had wrung from the plasma every possible snippet of information, he evaluated the mass of data he had accumulated. It convinced him that plasma transfusion would work. But there was only one way he could be certain—he would have to try actual plasma transfusion on humans.

Confronting Scudder with his findings, Drew made a detailed explanation of his conclusions and his proposal to transfuse plasma alone into patients whose illnesses did not specifically require replenishment of their red cells. It was a bold plan, but it had been solidly conceived, and all of Drew's experimental findings were persuasive. Testing was authorized by the hospital board. Plasma transfusion was undertaken on victims of massive burns and severe wounds. The plasma transfusions worked! A new era in blood transfusion dawned.

The medical world congratulated Charlie Drew on his brilliant breakthrough. Unlike whole blood, plasma did not have to be typed, because it had been stripped of the red cells that divide blood into separate groupings. Because plasma is 91 percent water, it could easily be preserved by removing its water and storing the compact, dried residue, and merely adding sterile water to the dried plasma prior to transfusion. This not only reduced storage space dramatically, it also eliminated the need for refrigeration. Other hospitals began establishing their own blood banks based on the Drew techniques. In recognition of his outstanding accomplishment, Columbia awarded him the doctor of science degree.

Dr. Drew's breakthrough could not have come at a time when it was more sorely needed. It was now 1940 and Europe was convulsed by World

War II. Battlefields and bombed cities were being stained red by their enormous quantities of casualties. The need for life-saving transfusions was massive and it was immediate. A cable arrived for Drew from London. It was signed by his old friend, John Beattie, who had become a director of the Royal Air Force medical service. Beattie asked if Drew would at once undertake to provide dried plasma to England, while British authorities organized their own blood banks modeled after his.

The response to this plea to help save lives was never in doubt. Dr. Drew immediately undertook the effort, securing facilities for processing the blood, gathering and training a team of technicians, supervising the entire operation. Within the next few months he succeeded in preparing and airlifting 5,000 units of dried plasma to the deeply grateful British.

With the war spreading and worsening, the United States was now deeply concerned with strengthening its own defense posture. The U.S. military authorities asked the American Red Cross to establish a plasma bank to support the military's medical resources. Choosing New York as the site for its first plasma bank, the Red Cross turned to Dr. Drew to head it up.

In early 1941 the federal government asked the Red Cross to expand its New York bank into a full-scale national blood-bank program. Dr. Drew was named medical director of this vast undertaking and at once plunged into the complexities of organization and operation.

If there was one thing that Charlie Drew had learned beyond all shadow of doubt during his years of probing the nature of blood, it was that—in human terms—the color of this vital body fluid is always and forever unchangeably red, only red. But now the military and the Red Cross insisted that blood was also "white" or "black," and ordered that all blood banked in the national system must be segregated according to the race of the donor, with plasma from white donors being used only for transfusing whites and plasma from blacks only for blacks. He and his medical staff were outraged, not only because the decision was morally inexcusable but because it was scientifically indefensible. Dr. Drew could not, either on the basis of scientific truth or in the interest of justice, support such an irrational position. Resigning his post as director of the Red Cross Blood Bank Program, he returned to Howard University's medical faculty. But he left in place the foundation for a nationwide blood-bank system that would, using the techniques he had pioneered, save countless thousands of lives.

Charlie Drew did not permit himself to become imprisoned by the hurt and the sorrow he felt. He knew that eventually truth and reason must triumph over blind prejudice and that segregation of blood by race must eventually be abandoned, as indeed it later was. In the meantime he continued to take on the heavy workload he had been accustomed to all of his life. He taught surgery at Howard, assumed direction of its department of surgery, lectured before medical groups, and probed on his own for answers to blood's remaining secrets. In 1944, he also assumed the responsibilities of chief of the professional staff of Washington's Freedmen's Hospital.

In 1949 the military authorities got in touch with Dr. Drew once again. Would he, they asked, inspect its hospitals, especially examining their surgical standards and procedures and making recommendations for their improvement? Notwithstanding the irony of this request from the Department of Defense, he undertook the mission willingly. He had never been one to penalize the ill for the shortcomings of the healthy.

On March 31, 1950, Charlie Drew worked his usual full schedule, spending much of the day performing surgery at Freedmen's Hospital. In the early evening he picked up three of the hospital's doctors, and the quartet set out on the long drive to Tuskegee Institute in Alabama to attend that famed black college's annual medical conference. Driving steadily, they stopped only to take turns behind the wheel. As dawn was beginning to lighten the night sky, the car was approaching Greensboro, North Carolina. Drew was once again in the driver's seat while his three companions dozed.

The way the state troopers later reconstructed it, Dr. Drew—so tired by his long day of surgery and his long night of driving—must also have dozed off for a minute. A minute was all it took. The car veered off the road, bounced across a ditch, overturned, and plowed to a halt in underbrush. Two of the passengers were bruised and shaken up. The third suffered a broken arm. But the driver sustained massive injuries.

An ambulance rushed Charlie Drew to the Greensboro Hospital. The staff sprang into action, working frantically. On instructions from the doctor in charge, a technician began a plasma transfusion, unaware that she was employing a technique that the patient himself had placed in her hands. Nothing helped. That body, still muscular and taut, had been damaged beyond repair. At the age of forty-six, Dr. Charles R. Drew died.

Index

The Author

Vernon Pizer is the author of two popular books from Putnam's— *You Don't Say: How People Communicate Without Speech* and *Ink, Ark., And All That: How American Places Got Their Names.* A free-lance writer, he is the author of several other books and more than 300 articles in major publications. Mr. Pizer entered the Army in World War II, serving in North Africa and Europe, and retired from military service as a lieutenant colonel in 1963. He and his wife live in Washington, D.C.